BETWEEN
THE
SHADOW
AND THE
SOUL

BETWEEN THE SHADOW AND THE SOUL

RANDOM POEMS

Frances Garrett Connell

authorHOUSE®

AuthorHouse™ LLC
1663 Liberty Drive
Bloomington, IN 47403
www.authorhouse.com
Phone: 1-800-839-8640

Published by AuthorHouse 12/04/2013

ISBN: 978-1-4918-3588-3 (sc)
ISBN: 978-1-4918-3587-6 (hc)
ISBN: 978-1-4918-3586-9 (e)

Library of Congress Control Number: 2013920964

TABLE OF CONTENTS

To the pursuit of justice and peace and a sustainable world, in which all may live, aware of their obligations to seven generations to come.

Truth is both static and dynamic . . . the one does not exist without the other. It is no simple task to stand on a mountaintop and at the same time see details of the valley, and details are not mere accidents.

-Gerald Casey, Welsh poet

Poetry's grammar, structure and language have their own wisdom— entering its woods we find ourselves living with thought forms that feed only with the ways of the leafy and hidden.

-Jane Hirshfield, *Nine Gates*

I

NEW SHADOWS

LUCKY AS A NIGHT BARISTA AT TEASM

☙ ❧

(After *Waiting for Godot*)

Hot brews shatter my muteness,
dispersing drinks from the bar,
scooping dry teas from glass bottles
like captured Amoy ships,
I hear everything again.

But habit is a great deadener, he told Gogo
after I led my blind master away
to take up my night job.

Under track lights, bald pate glistens
mirroring pewter pots, porcelain cups,
hands dance across samovar and faucet,
smile shellacs tables where
people bend sipping heat.

If they ask, I counsel:
Young Hyson tempts nakedness,
Lung Ching Dragonwell burns lips.
I sell solace in Silvertop Yin Hao,
romance in Jasmine,
oblivion, memory in the Sencha.

Still they take their chances
with the Hao Yo Keemun,
gab as I filter the Lapsing Souchang,
giggle over old maid shots—
Earl Grey, Orange Pekoe.

Frances Garrett Connell

Few reflect on English treachery
flooding Chinese markets with Indian Opium
addicting the poor to fill home-savored teacups.

Time passes:
no older then contemplated leaves,
a pot full of residue,

or the rope that burns in the man's hand
for whom I bear the bags
all my days.

LOST AND FOUND

ᘒ ᘒ

We've come to the wrong place.
-Becket: **Waiting for Godot**

We've come to the wrong place
to this injured shade's stunted branches
a crucified pirouette holding
chained blue jays and cardinals.

> *We've waited years for a tree to come down*
> *to bridge the banks at the foot of our hill*
> *laying its poplar barked longitude*
> *across latitudes of cold creek.*

We've toe-heeled through mud
to loquacious mutes and blind seers
in rooms where dollars cushioned
the torn cradles of buried children.

> *We've attended raucous rains,*
> *pelting downpours, owl-hooting,*
> *crow-calling winds, fierce sun shouts,*
> *midnight stark star silence.*

We've dressed in rough silks
donned stoneware berets
danced in ballet slippers cased in granite
limped through each marathon.

> *We've bent ourselves hesitant and clean*
> *at dawn birdsong choruses,*
> *traced bones and lips when*
> *timbers' hairy chests heaved and swayed.*

We've stippled the green lawn,
galloped over stenciled fences
to sing our own diseased homage,
to sip thimbles of fog.

> *We've wakened to discordant lullabies*
> *sensed tangled roots, splay shoots*
> *unearthing from feeble clay ravine.*

We've come, emptied,
seeking burnt memories:
but the place is wrong

> *Now, this trunk leans down,*
> *a gentle giant clasping each bank*
> *calling us to cross, one to the other again.*

Pilgrim and soldier,
we chew the thick air,
the circle squared.

ODE TO THE ELDER

ை ஒ

"Let us not waste our times in idle discourse . . .
Let us do something while we have the chance.
-Becket: **Waiting for Godot. Act. II**

We are Moorish Arab, Sephardi Jew,
Prague gypsy, Irish bard
teasing the sitar, lute, fiddle, cello:
all hollow-bellied stringed creatures sighing.

Pale silver eyebrows arch
over caramel-pebbled eyes,
shiny as newly washed stones:
they pelt my face at eye-level.

As you tease, I imagine
a tiny boy pulling back a rubber band:
lobbing wadded arithmetic paper
into a coy girl's inkwell.

You conjure cardinals
yellow chickadees out of season
flutter red maple branches:
night's crest-tipping raven wings,

string beads to light the wooden houses
mirrored in inky Lake Anna,
mull a sweet German wine:
under fluid-eyed Walter Russell [1]sculptures.

---

[1]   An American artist and mystic known for his achievements as a painter, sculptor, author and builder and less well known as a natural philosopher and for his unified theory in physics and cosmology (1871-1963).

Your kibitzing warms better
than the daily hot oatmeal
my Texas grandfather swore brought immorality,
carries me across Europe's stone-laced villas on your handlebars.

Meeting you is like swaying in a pub sing
bold voices belting out sea shanties:
willowy plaids entwining,
when I'd only known dark café corners.

Or being seated beside a stranger
who's reading the same book
we two parallel, silent:
your tale referenced in the volume before me.

Memory, an acquired taste,
we touch its texture,
leave years,
the bones and threads, intact.

"Frozen in Fear"

෧෨ ෭෨

Water from springs,
snow melt,
scant summer rain,
creates high altitude lakes
luring migratory flamingos
to roost.

On frigid nights
ice forms like lace
around their legs:

the morning sun
sets them free.

-Description of the Azmain of Chile,
a high desert between the Andes and the Pacific.

DADDY'S BATHROOM MANNERS

Why my father left the door open,
the lights off,
mystified me,
those nights he rose in the dark

to use the toilet
or when he'd scuttle in tattered pj's
long past retiring,
to the bathroom:

water entering the bowl
thundered on my teenage ears
his form crossing the hall by my bedroom
wounded.

He, child of Victorian parents
stentorian in verbal thrusts
sloppy suited and shuffling,
urinated

as if to call us forth
to hear, too see,
to understand

what?

IN A REAL POET'S SALON

Among post-menopausal *femme fatales*
flowery tunic-topped widows,
black-haired grandmothers,
and adoring interlopers

the handlebar-mustached poet
sashays knowing giggles
from gadflies' throats
and buzzing bees on the wall.

Silence refines my voice:
I slip on the role of mourner
like a sacred pinafore.

In this circle
they see through veils
and lead.

I do not shout.

II

CONNECTION

WAITING

෯෧෨ ෧෨

Stark's at the end of the steel, was as ugly as proud flesh.
-Wallace Stegner
(for John Snow[2])

Steeped in miasma and sighs
we don't dare turn too inward
over one small mortality.

The gentle Dr. Snow, crease-browed virgin and vegetarian,
tilts bald crown, strokes beard like a rough sketch
and waits, twenty-two years,

frock-coated, waistcoats rippling, front bibbed,
he snaps a bow tie around steel stiff collars,
and dispels untethered theories,

rues that parasite-rich brew
spreads and blooms in swallowed water
to harvest the living.

Orating shyly at the Medical Society on
"Asphyxia and the Resuscitation of New-born Children,"
he ingests, tests anesthesia's volatile fumes to eliminate sensitivity.

Admitted to the Queen's bedroom,
her life, the birth of princes, trusted to his hands,
he knocks her out with chloroform
he understands so well.

---

[2]   *In 1854 an epidemic of cholera killed over 600 people in London, as part of a cycle of the disease.*

That September, when 600 redden, chaff
in St. Anne's Place, he wades through Soho's cowsheds,
past slaughterhouses, to survey ancient cesspools,

chart rooms, workhouses, and crowded cellars,
their air drenched in boiling grease,
to the water's source,

traces death to a sick child's wrung nappies
tipped into a leaking sewer, feeding
the fatal epicenter, the Broad Street pump.

Days later the parish guardian grips
the end of the steel, removes the pump handle:
and the epidemic ends.

Eighteen years more they wait,
those Victorians with a pompous lack of logic,
to swallow the German germ theory of disease.

Dr Snow,
we still wait for antidotes
to displace miasmas,

someone to see the obvious and act—
lift the lever,
remove our current plagues.

SEEKING MIRACLES

Focus, abandon
will and grace
lead to the center, to memory.

Read it well,
the finger pointing
is not the same
as the object pointed at.

Drop everything you expect
then let your eyes see
what waits to be seen.

Out of an underground cave
language unknowingly
raises heart and its motions,

thought born here
climbs to the brain,
silently becomes insights

intelligence
only then journeys outward
in words.

If we smother heart language
with ready-made ideas

we are not listening.

EXISTENTIALS

❧ ❧

(Tashkurghan, Afghanistan,
February, 1974)

Across the room Tom laughs
"Oh yes, we could coin a phrase . . ."

I've just said something
about our Peace Corps cook
how we were dealing with an artist of sorts
how I admire someone
who can create with food,
how it's really a kind of existential act
since all the work
passes away again.

"Oh yes," he grins,
that Irish ruthlessness ablaze.
"Right down
the old existential funnel

of existence . . ."

SVETLANA'S OTHER DAUGHTER

After a Kazakhstan school bus skidded over barriers,
stacked like timber
in a country where protests burned illegal,

her Russian-bowed 10-year old
dropped at the Tian Shah Children's Camp
wasted into fever only days after she arrived,

brought home
just in time for burial,
causes eternally unknown,

the institute professor, an oval-eyed mother
stretched her pained body over
the 5-year old daughter left behind,

taught her fear, suspicion, anger,
imprinted in her the need to dissemble
to survive.

FOUR QUIPS

၆ၖ ၛၜ

(From *The Writer Observed* by Harvey Breit

E.M. Forster, he claimed, was
*altogether looking like a spare
intelligent, ruffled heron.*

Christopher Morley:
*as intelligent
as any thin man.*

He echoes Nietzsche's claim:
*perhaps all vulgarity consisted
in man's inability to resist stimuli.*

Or, that:
*the mind must learn to think
as a form of dance.*

Pound, he recalls, thought:
*what matters is not the idea a man holds
but the depth at which he holds it.*

While T.S. Eliot found:
*the main difference between
the good and the bad poet*

*was not so much one of talent,
as it was the inability of the bad poet
to be unconscious at the right times.*

ROPES

I needed the ropes, she kept telling me.

Not for special effects,
holding up actors in movies,
dancing them from roof to courtyard
until the final scene, their halters gone,
they fly.

I kept my ropes on me
lapped one piece over the other

tied one side only
after I'd finished the first.

We coil them so they won't kink,
flemished, singed,
or bound the ends with twine tape
to prevent fraying.

Ropes bear tensile strength:
pull but not push,
twisted and braided fiber
to connect,
skeins fed into winches and capstans.

Childhood taunted, exhaled,
the ropes key to our games:

Every dawn,
the venetian blinds' long cotton cords
flipped up, slates spun to open straight,
edging in the world outside;
at night, dropping the curtains on light.

Sisal rope swings on oak trees,
so tall we'd leap to the seat running,
clutch airy pendulum.
Jump ropes turning spun coils faster and faster,
slapping asphalt newly bridging ditches.

The fat rope dangling from the gym vaults,
we'd wrap our legs around,
scoot up like sailors on stormy mastheads
high as light fixtures and heated rafters
to win blue ribbons for "Top of the Rope."

Later, three sheets to the wind,
we'd sail, manning jib-sheet, cleated halyard,
raising, lowering the mast
skating up the river, our lines,
controlling everything.

I needed the ropes,
each innocent's gamble,

blended cotton, linen,
manila hemp, or sisal,

held me in air or water
raised me for decades
from dead ground.

GREETING SINGLE MALE ERITREAN REFUGEES
AT REAGAN NATIONAL AIRPORT

They come
callow as my own sons
hawk-sharp eyes watching,
cheeks hollow, travel weary,
skin still dusty from Shimelba Camp,
yoked with the IOM[3] badges,
their identities around their necks.

Slowly, they enter
as I wait beyond Airport Security,
hold a lettered sign with their name wilting,
motion them to enter the tunnel
to the terminal
smile, extend hands:
Welcome to this land.

They've escaped military thugs,
stolen from middle school a decade ago
forced to fight for Somalian warlords,
Sudanese merchant armies,
made to man the desert-ripped border
with Ethiopia
from which a wife, a brother earlier fled.

---

[3] Transport for each refugee admitted to the U.S. is arranged by the International
Migration Organization (IMO).

Or, one of the trio,
brothers together here by different means:
the oldest entered on a fellowship
two decades before
found work and stayed,
the second smuggled through the middle passage
Qatar, South America, Baltimore,

this last escaped from a refugee camp
a four-by-four-foot tent shared with eight others
dust, dirty water, heat, TB
inhaled on Sudan's desolate plains
in Sita wo'ishrin,
Wedisherifay
and Shegerab.

They seek the simplest:
work, school, housing,
their families, pain's end.

Behind chiseled cheekbones,
huge black eyes
stare at another distant light.

AVEBURY COMPLEX, ENGLAND

Coming dark and sleek
between posted signs
and chained doors
fury battles its wings

remembering what was left undone
breathing and smarting
on that windy day
the clergy found themselves booted.

It's Wiltshire and the Hedge sprawls:
tangling serpent, rain-smoothed
skeleton of wind-chiseled stones
among hills and barrows.

Giant rocks loom; they are
flat women carved in the earth
megaliths un-swathed
to seek energy,

they sword fight the curving plain
ripple streams and ponds across fields
from wide circles
turned to open temples.

Petrified fecundity:
these are women
hard as steel.

RECONNECTING IN GREAT FOLDS

Odd isn't it, she told me,
writing 30 years after college,
*the things that go away
somehow come back.*

On route to his school
where I introduced her to Stephan
the year his father died in the NASA crash,
we'd rehearsed the same lines.

Now, a widow, she takes his call each week
the shattered physics professor in Calgary
whose own marriage gives him nothing
but matched socks.

Their dark young heads plotting,
debating Sanskrit, Zen and Black Holes.
Now hair autumn streaked,
sultry Armenia floats, dark Holland graces.

Energy convulsed on itself
in dark holes,
great folds.

OUT OF SYNC AT AN IRISH WEDDING

Garbed in green velveteen gown,
mid-calf cut classic

lacking only coquette silk bows
over warm ears,
where tiny pearl clip-ons glow

she catches her image, starts,
too girlish for a 50-year old, a lawyer's wife,
in this company of business women's woolens,
net bodices, and designer looks.

She beams at two family friends, turned seven,
who float among the guests,
like hungry butterflies.

BEDROCK

ঙ্ক ৵ ৵

If you take the *ji-chu* from Chinese
blend it to make a *qiao*
you get a word for *bedrock, foundation.*

Out of such twisted ideograms
I'd thought to root a family tree
build up from buried basements
walls holding back two rivers.

It was 1967.
Sundays to weave the day, practice my Chinese words
I walked Broadway from Columbia to its source

past excavations on the bounded superlot.
Vesey, Liberty, Church and West
braced a soggy hole
to plummet 70 feet

We saw only the building's parts
sketched out like mist
rigid hollow tubes, closely spaced steel columns.
floor trusses in a central core,
silver aluminum.

You joined me once,
hugged my childish, childless form
against explosive cityscapes

as wind jerked our woolen shoulders
(though you never wore a coat),
blew back my hair so my round globe,
unblemished face, glowed.

We gasped at the gales
turning tops in the canyons of Wall Street,
on the Ferry we yielded
to water and the plowed sheath.

My Chinese floundered
I gave up the study
never reached the level of one who knows

foundation comes from *groundwork*
that *bedrock*, the solid rock,
holds in it also
"bad," hard," inflexible."

Fearful the racing elevators,
the dense pressured air
would buckle conventional shafts
they had made the Towers without masonry.

The week before their bombing
you met a client in No. 2,
five months later
you were both gone.

From our foreign cities now,
we look into holes.

RONDEAU

"Scientist slow speed of light to pace of Sunday drive."
-Headline in *The Washington Post,* February 23, 1999.

We chisel words, tight as hammered nails
our motions delve and rise, now fail
to catch a vowel in its climb,
cleaver the rhythms in their time
        to purge the world of everything it ails.

Question one spare, rare adjective retells
just how emphatic energy prevails
we pitch a lexicon of rhyme
pour pitch to roof the boards of metered line
        to purge the world of everything it ails.

United, the form takes over from the frail
demands a name, a syntax and a sail,
we counter with a springing line to climb
finish the exercise, a scripted paradigm
        to purge the world of everything it ails.

ANNIVERSARY POEM FOLLOWING MOTHER'S DEATH

ॐ ॐ

(For Tom, 34 Years to the Wind, Sunshine and Rain)

I.
You came through,
as you had said you would,
squeezed yourself into a dawn flight,
after gently launching me once, twice, to my mother's side,

braved Houston heat, greedy traffic,
gawking relatives hungry for your phrases and roses,
Christian inflections on eternity and forgiveness,
(stomached a whole day of Southerners at prayer)

to wander alone in your farewells to her,
this eternal mother we shared
among Findeisen, Ashorn and Garrett headstones,
white rose sprays and early summer lilacs and zinnias,

to a country cemetery in New Ulm's orb,
wedged by Industry, Wesley and Brenham's
curving green pastures,
bared red clay gullies,

to stand beside me,
our East coast family in tailored black suits,
your oldest sons shouldering a head above you,
the youngest absent in his solitude.

You came through,
gifted me with your promise fulfilled
as you had in so many settings,
over trenchant years.

II.
At another service,
at the church where we married 34 years ago,
red poppies, tulips, roses, mums
blazoned Pentecostal walls, as a world of people spoke:

large-boned Dakota minister wept
through Corinthians, the Psalms,
a soprano soared with hymns
on many-roomed mansions, gardens, cleaving rocks,

Brother Dan strummed guitar,
breathed aching song
of Tibetan exiles
needing to return,

a Himalayan scholar declaimed his dream:
imagined a newborn baby girl reincarnated,
the white infant shoes hugging the curb
he'd seen the morning Mother passed.

Elsie, caretaker from North St. Louis streets,
sobbed for a lost friend,
mumbled thanks for the privilege
of serving a feisty elder's memories.

Generous professor, Anne-Sophie
shared humor, teacups and family stories,
praised an adopted grandmother
whose calls gave her *"a scream" and "a trip"*

as the Taoist half-Chinese
grandson Warren celebrated
caregivers, time's cycles,
refined souls, and hope.

III.
I stood for all of us,
mute from the magic and finality
like her blood
that surges through our children,

a smile that lightened midnight quivers,
walked lone pathways,
modesty that wondered why we bothered,
a faith that wanted brokenness to heal.

Notes from Jerome Bruner's

On Knowing: Essays for the Left Hand

ॐ ॐ

1.
How clever he put it, Mr. Bruner:
Sequence is a fiction
and in a human life
what follows
may produce what went before.

Just so,
with one you've never met
you find already
a history of your friendship
in images tersely shared

a hoarded dark chocolate bar, fresh watermelon,
wrung tears for a massacre in Norway
the Mississippi winding past a house
a bike ride as the sun sets
soft colors singing in holy arbors overhead

in the fear: a son resettled two continents away
or mindfulness:
pedaling's sweat and pull up a mountain
finding we'd both done it in the same city,
three weeks apart, on visits to other sons.

in marriages ended,
nine years ago.

2.
Was it a quote
also from Bergman
affirming how time was first
the invisible progress of the past
in the evaluation of the future?

Aren't we time-walking, half a country apart?

3.
It goes out from the theorists:
a firm shoulder grip,
a touch not permitted a stranger,
intuition, a mind and spirit dissatisfied
with too much of the disciplined.

I want to run to the top of a grassy hill,
roll down like a butter churn in "The Three Little Pigs,"
stretch tummy down and tickle someone
stand in the street wobbling a hula hoop
giggle, hug, unpredictable as puppies.

We define ourselves by what we create,
seek for pleasure, narrate,
learn, empower, judge,
how we use our bodies, fear death.

4.
So can two people

as Bruner categorized—
one sustained by stories, drama, specific details,
the other logically constructing propositions, paradigms—

blend in as one?

I'D RATHER . . .

I'd rather tell you how Van Gogh stars
hovered overhead
as I ran the neighborhood
circling nightly miles

of apple pie bread conjured from scratch
lingering like warm nurturing arms
above the labyrinthine rooms of this beloved house
filling lean stomachs with good grain and flavor

or of the longing, pride
as I read your finely-honed words
about selkies,
the foots of bed,
loved sons,
passages over time,

I'd rather laugh with you over
our youngest son helping his studious friend with his
"Me, the Celebrity" school assignment,
how our little director dressed and filmed and postured

the diffident and awkward teen as a punk rapper
who tossed hips and ten dollar bills (Monopoly)
as he jerked up and down stairs
with a false microphone and sound track.

I'd rather share the sweet peace in Renoir's faces
"Madame Monet and Her Son"
as your middle son and I talked our way
between absurdist blank canvases and nesting rooms

full of falling paper at the Hirshhorn,
Picasso's cubist fragmentation of Fernande Olivier,
the Impressionists' altars,
one stolen blue afternoon.

I'd rather send you chocolates,
richly soft, colored shirts and poems
floating above the hard reality of our distance
like captured cumulus clouds

pen in detail indulgent humor and pride
to celebrate each son's days and activities,
my own small successes,
or listen, trusted, to details of your hours,

help comb away like fallen hair, clipped nails
extraneous, outgrown parts of our life
share scintillating films, music and novels,
travel, comfort:

I'd rather
join you
in things
yet possible.

THE BENCH SITTER AT BATTERY PARK

She catches my eye lightly,
pedals on, legs pumping up and down
like the fountain's
      web by web, ripples racing
or the tilt-nosed turquoise tug boat
forcing the steel barge over the Hudson.

Quick as a sunbeam—
her comprehension.
dances on my foot, my shoulder
      as the oak tree's canopy
opens an instant
then closes over to shade—

She sees beyond this old man
shoulders sagged, mouth tucked in a pout
arms wrinkled as
      undulating sea
under green-striped polo,
legs still behind creased tan slacks.

Sees my youth, manhood
shinnying up the earth's roof
where air chokes, eyes sail into heaven:
      Nande Ders, Tirach Mir, Khula Kangar
in India, Afghanistan, Bhutan,
Lenin Peak, Huacarun, McKinley,

in Tajikistan, Peru, Alaska.
Commandeering porters and climbers,
geologists and bureaucrats
                to gather rocks, measure crevices,
chart altitudes, draw topography,
hunt out ancient trails.

Nights when the snow slathered us,
the parched avalanches hanging above,
days when the sun
                cut us into broiled strips
sucked away the water we sipped
like blood, we stayed.

Something she sees:
my eyes consume
the lay of the land
        still.

DAVID, 1943-1996

They are burning down your pine forest in Bastrup
a drought's sucked every moist drop for over a year
torches Texas, licks it lifeless as a tinderbox

while its governor labels global warming
a conspiracy, convenes prayers for God to
let the rain fall on his favored Anglo-Saxon flock.

You would have wept, depressed even more
to live to see the house you built,
stick by stick, go up in flames
sibilant shade melted into scorched earth,
streams dried up.

Only a few times in all your life,
I talked with you,
brother who quit the family at 18
returning home again at 33.

That week together in mother's old house,
we spoke of lost time,
your pre-med studies, a year of law school,
cultivating Emerson and Thoreau
in a shack on the Bay

mornings waking up
glued to the bed
losing jobs, wandering skid row hotels,
hanging out on welfare
and alcohol,

days reading in the library
taking in Catholic Charities,
Salvation Army retreats, food, advice
finding AA's solution,
but knowing it all,

preferring self-exile
craving to be superior in something
an expert in Shakespeare
or carpentry
or gardening

thinking to save money to buy a sailboat
to go around the world.

Once, moving your trailer load
in New York, New Jersey, California,
the trailer unhitched.
You set the whole thing ablaze,
all you had in the world,

gloriously watched it burn
beside the night road.

You feared all cycles.
In a Lone State bar
you once bet an old professor
your life for his,
after he'd lost wife, job, desire to live

concluding men
who spent a life doing the "worthwhile"
still face final misery.

Alcohol put strange words in your mouth
so one night you found yourself weeping
terrified in a police court
for violent things said
to a stranger.
Over and over, divorced from society
animal or plant life
you thought you were not human

saw no sense in even discussing it
convinced yours was a fatal disease,
you didn't want attempts
at reaching peace
shattered before that death.

In those days we talked,
you feared going out, wielding a hammer
making noise, even
timed your garbage emptying
to night or early morning

so as not to be seen,
rehearsed every motion
from waving atop the driveway
to offering neighbors the garden's
overflow tomatoes.

In your dark room
your always present cigarette glowing
you sat wearily on your bed,
admitted sparing distrusted psychiatrists,
the facts on our family, your death-will.

You would not let me touch you either:
I listened in sorrowful love
glimpsing that macabre peace,
truth as dangerous,
fleeting as quicksilver.

You needed someone
to love you
into finding yourself,
an idea too simple
and simple you were not.

Fourteen years hence, yourself long buried,
I write out the callowness
as the Texas hills,
site of your brief reprieve,
fester and burn.

Mishmash Nightmare

Longing, on runner's arches
to flee the moil
josh instead of scold,
bend ungulated feet,
balance all forms on hoofed tip toes,

she raced the sketched chariot of her dream
around and around a hippodrome
as dry and sparse as the ancient world
in our sun-baked century.

Then lubricious stares coated the track,
undercut her balance, tripped her knees,
bowlegged her legs, salacious.

One man stood out, his gimlet eye speared,
so she swayed with his panache, then jactitated—
arms a whirling dervish, feet pulsing widely,
body gyrating,
left with the cicatrice, puffy flesh unsoothed.

Above her head clouds postured,
sand caught in rain made gristly,
the fields crinkled with early spring,
diurnal light oblivious to thunder.

Diffident, she began to decipher,
her gestures stunted,
eyes slumbering like rai songs on the Rif,

when the sky was the glassy
green, blue and yellow of Rahalia plates in Fez,
magicians undulated on the Jeman el Fna,
tourists discerned geometric shapes
on Atlas cedar woods

among tajines, teapots, passing sellers and shoppers
bodies shrouded in dusty burnoses and jellabas
while almond blossoms wafted from the orchards,
no part of the word or world
lay limpid.

IN A NEW YORK APARTMENT, MARCH 2011

Out the window

light brush strokes
stark branches shadow Beaux-Arts
the acorn-hatted water tower
perches on the square pedestal
ten stories up

my own house was never warm

here I sleep year round
under one layer

III

EROS'S ERRORS

DARK SOUL[4]

࿐ ࿐

I send you *duende**
lavender and rose twined in seductive brown,
like Andalusian guitars skating night winds
gathering skirts, shawls, potent as matador capes
before the burnt passion of the bull's silken rout.

I send you *duende,*
red blood, black soil, light flickering
uncoiled in mirroring iris, hung under
moon spears as they plow earth's pregnant rows of pain,
mime's cant, picking blackbird feathers from seeded ground.

I send you *duende*
supplicant hands folded, ivory palm
tending splay-leg, fired breast,
puckered and full-lipped, as rain pelts worn ravines
in your keystoned archways.

I send you *duende:*
ocean's sand-mist to color light streaked into wounds,
breezes to strum summer grass's harp
clear hazel Rembrandt eyes to glaze each shadow day,
one rushing creek whose canopies scream joy.

I send you, *duende:*
hear, smell, heed
your own,
laugh, you dark soul.
No one suspects the days to be gods.[5]

---

[4]   After Garcia Lorca's essay on "duente."

[5]   Emerson

Frances Garrett Connell

LABYRINTH

❧ ❧

*"Midway this way of life we're bound upon
I woke to find myself in a dark wood,
Where the right road was wholly lost and gone."*
-Dante

Follow the fetal string
back to the red-lipped pulse
where wary shadows slip across gullies
fabled as brocaded silks.

Knots dance along beveled axis
ribboned turns and starts
between centripetal and centrifugal spirals
elegantly intertwined as fugues.

Satin threads bind thin fingers
pummel soles against unscaled walls
pause between rings and links
follow canal and invertible to sound inner ears.

The labyrinth, a double ax
curls on itself like the cochlea's tiny spiral
revolves around daisy petal's snowy prints
plucked from the pistil's seeded stigma and style.

50

Mime the meandering,
paths stretch impassable
to the place a red heart languishes
snared in tangled arteries of exit.

Boldly vanquish the beast
beat with butterfly wings,
unwinding Ariadne's thread.

Take the bull by the horns
and enter.

SHOWERS

All the time the shower thundered
you shed your seed
held all night in our bed's chilly frame
where your weary snoring
drove me to pokes and back-sided glares
until morning tonic braced your skin.

Staggering,
we moved in obligations
in this vault
I had no patience, you no trust,
so you took the dry plain,

tossed out everything
without culling.

To a Man I Would Will to Look Up

The blood has returned to the leaves:

film frozen oval suns
orange palms sheeting the sky
thrust limbs stripped to bare brown
on paths mute with the first fall.

It was always your season
your birthright, clear October mornings
when we hungered young,
air vibrant as a Sistine ceiling
creation's spark lifting limbs to bind.

The ghosts of the 6,000 silent women
raped in Berlin by the occupying Russians
pause in the breeze six decades late.
They grandmother frail girls in a world
as toxic as their pain,
frame stories about someone else's violation.

But looking up,
crisp titian sky
meandering clouds morph heaven,
or hell's abyss:
your eyes mirror hazel haunting.

Unseasoned, outstretched fingers
left from spring
paint naked longing
on a woman suspended.

Each turning blush wills
dead-leafed winter's end.

INVITATION

❦ ❦

Tuck me under lapel's lip
among wiry tuff disclosing your neck
in navel's phantasmagoria and silky bristle
crawling beneath bent arms, around mount.

Let me garnish your shoulders with flushed skin
comb though your hair with sipping lips
clutch your waist close in last belt notch
clasp buttonhole just above your heart.

Nestle me in invisible cuff links
rounding your wrists
watching among elastic band
trailing in the hem of your trousers.

Slither me up the split of your pant legs
into the cup of your restraint
sheltered from wind's sharp teeth
walled snow, and knuckled night's fists.

Let me flow all over
softly as fallen light
enter and share
flesh's shine.

Why I Took My Clothes Off for
My Husband

☙ ❧

Over and over it came
all winter long between
Christmas and the vernal equinox.

In the dream you stand
a lean amoeba-riddled traveler
whittled to skeleton and eyes.

You clasp your hands in front,
a basket cupped tightly
full of milky seed.

The day hangs hotly,
my steps dawdle, dry as fall stalks
as we hike above some snaking gorge,

silently, moving higher up a valley.
Each time we pause
you offer me two cradling hands for drink

and I drink, tender back
fold fingers, an Indian *namaste,*
like a chancel's peaked roof.

In the dream under greenery loud with spring
sheet bleached fleecy clouds
un-damned azure sky

we fold ourselves among swaying rushes
a nightingale warbles soft as lambs wool
wind meanders dry webs around old distances.

A fresh river, you begin: at the arch of my sole
dance fingers pliant and silky as pussy willow
up legs like ivory ladders

glide over breasts delta
to ruby pockets of pomegranate jewels
up, up past child couching stomach

around Gibraltars of bone-struck pelvis
to two warm fountains
gurgling with sable heat and honey,

up, up to the carved clavicle
the un-scarved neck
to chin, lips, eye, hair.

In the dream I swallow you whole
you drink from me,
up, up, through the hollow rib cage

and back to my heart.

PROSE POEM AFTER THE GREEKS:
DRAFT ONE

☙ ❧

If I can not stroke your ivory fingers,
cup you red flare buried pulse,

if it is not my hands that daily plow
sheaves of your tame hair
or walk the bone of your nose,
cavern of eye socket, hot velvet lips,

if the ache that arches
to companion your enclaves,
touches empty air on my dusky runs
beneath windows of coupled and coupling,

if my brown haven eyes,
round, silent, close,
shunted from shining into yours
(yet know your spectral,
what attracts and repels,
pace the peace as one who understands),

if I can not warm myself
beside the hot stove of your tactile skin,
coax and comb the feathery silk
that beards your bearings,

if I may not daily tender hard words, laugh queries,
postpone pauses, with scintillating kiss,
phrase, certainty and presence—

Still,
the leaves fall,
coins shaken from banking trees
muted by the months,

yet
your smell, touch, taste clings,
perennials and evergreens
in seasons-shaking woodland,
V-phalanx of winter geese gliding
year after year toward February suns,

web of my hand, our rivers,
blazed
on pale palms,
branded
on threaded throats

enduring as breath itself.

AFTER THE GREEK, II

No, I do not peel a fresh petal every morning,
blood-red as pricked fingers and speared palm,
from the rose of our hallowed years
and frightful mourning.

I hesitate and fail to carve out words
quick as mirror-caught sun's flash
in messages left behind
long after your eyes and body
have closed down with sleep,
in your exiled rooms,

And
the nails I drag across the slate of my hurried learning,
smudge like rubrics glyphed in fall's tenuous language—
swirled and fallen leaves
across stretched blue sky, green-spiked lawn
where capering creatures arch and scold
with the resilience of honeyed mead.

Yet
I daily plant an orchard,
gather elegant named bouquets,
harvest each spun-off veil—
absent and lost—

ready to flower tomorrow.

First Awake in the Late '90s

I could not face into you
our lardy forms repel
like poled magnets

I stretched for the warm spot
between bodies
linen pressed in us
along mattress, fluted coverlet,
where strained truces
snarled passion's imprint

Back in Brown Hall
Princeton, 1968
I think how the silent bat

hovered
on the door portico
outside your room
come home like a puffy chapel bell.

Cold under both sets of blankets
I grab for the wall
the window, light's crack.

A year later your smell lingers
the thinnest strand of your hair
hides in the winter bedspread's folds
an English green garden that topped our bed,
curtained our windows
these fifteen years.

Death doesn't sit in your stomach
like a fine dinner
it gnaws in your veins

pulsates into capillaries
moves to arteries, muscles, heart,

as does absence.

It is June.
I am tired
of being brave.

An Indiscreet Fantasy, Which is Also a Poem

There is a fire in the valley
flames surging, licking the velvet brown delta

from which three lives flowed
singeing either side of this internal river.

Voices, too many words, clamor,
wind tongues dry brush,

whispers sizzle, a blazing beehive
up from a buried nest among felled trees.

A fire between the mountains
strokes lunar skin still soft as a schoolgirl's.

I flood raging heat and light,
deluges worthy of a Noah's ark.

Only the touch of your salty wand
can qualm the flames.

FANTOUM, IMPERFECTED

෨ ෨

And if we skirted everyday to savor far away
eyes, hands, licked from fertile black-seeded poppies
while easy bound to land
hazy as the Hudson this July twilight
the lie between us always shadow.

Hugged, cotton burrs inseparate as a lover's smell
eyes cavorting in rivers silhouetted far away
soothed fear as rain-basked shadow
to pass a seamless afternoon to twilight
arms snug around waist, unwounded poppies
could we navigate each other's land?

A rusty barge inches forward between green land
fresh lavender courts with heresy's smell
from a Riverside bench I watch one player until twilight
you're on a trip with friends never faraway
unseeing, would you scoff at carpets thick with poppies
that move across my history like shadow?

A misty breeze springs, dancers in shadow
I imagine your touch, solid as land.
In line for pity, veterans sold paper poppies,
inside their shirts a Mercurochrome smell
troubled lovers saunter far away
pause along the river before twilight.

Would you wrap around me, light at twilight
hold me close as cushioned shadow
whisper a postponed trip to faraway
garnish prickled skin, my dry land
show rivers lapping around your smell,
warm lips holding poppies?

Our smiles break, crystal poppies
what rowed across the river is twilight
limbs, legs afloat like smell
as we twin in arbor's shadow
neighbors bang down dominoes from other lands
starved by fear, we'll nibble far away.

I glow:
each cheek candled poppies
cast in shadowy twilight

Illuminated like lands and maps
each keen word fresh seed to smell
I reach across to touch your faraway.

TRYING ON AN OLD LOVE

⟋⟍ ⟍⟋

(for JLP)

Of course, I will love you to the end of time:

For
the sweet kiss spread on my cheek
as the credits rolled for "Cat Ballou."
Your taut wrestler's torso
inching my skinny chest,
you picked up my hand like melting ice
and grinned at me, our first date.

For
walks down Blackberry Lane and Hanley
as I clutched leaning towers of books
decades before everyone carried backpacks.
You matched my bird-darting steps,
joking about "Our Town," Dostoevsky,
Mr. Sander's bumbling chemistry class puns,

Miss Rothchild's tigress composition standards,
Miss Henry's punishment for couples holding hands,
my note to you that got me—
always Little Miss Goody Two Shoes—
thrown out of Mrs. Epstein's pre-cal class,
your colleagues in the brain trust,
Mark, Tony and Steve
perpetually objects of my crushes

those afternoons in high school
when the world still waited.

For
finding me 40 years later
both of us with broken wings
from long marriages,
caged expectations,
both of us with three sons.

For
dining in the Georgetown cafe
in my adopted Federal City.
Contented, a miner for souls,
you gently strayed,
up and down my emerald suit,
touching my arms, face, eyes
like some fairy godmother's wand.
as we shared Burgundy, spaghetti carbonara,
and life stories.

For
meeting me again,
in the native city you had never left:
where, candle glossed, we ate Portuguese
in a reclaimed stone factory
beside the frozen Mississippi,
dipped eclairs in chocolate,
tongues hot and sticky
to lap up dishes
like kittens their milk.

For
dancing, giddy under cutout stars
in a silent Saint Louis park,
as the car heater pumped
dispensing with protocol,
eons from awkward adolescent
pats and misses
setting mouth, legs, afire.

For
bringing us to this liquid April night,
(a flight shared, a marathon run),
to dine in shimmering medieval rooms
above a luminescent, bridge-looped Seine,
to a balcony over the Arc de Triomphe
to burrow into secrets

clearly wasted on the young.

IV

ANCIENT JOURNEYS

Boston's Saint E's

High-hilled, its brow squints over Brighton's streets.
plowed by the Green Line trolley
    from Commonwealth's split arteries

the steps from Cambridge, Warren and Nevin mount fiercely
to brick colonnade dorms and sheer white edifice that
    hunker and haunt.

This place where our mother, Claire of the light,
placed the decades-long dark nightmare:
    over and over:

footsteps sounding, a stranger shadowing
as she climbed to a student nurse's dorm,
    for her dawn-hungry shift.

Orderlies and interns in lime scrubs pace themselves
where stiff-capped nurses, herself among them,
    once rued straight-lines in their heavy white stockings,

rehearsed Latin names for medicines they'd mix themselves
under Sister's judging eyes and eagle-talon hands
    before doctors as lofty as Cabots and God.

Generations, stone-hearts remote
from the laywomen Third Order of St. Francis
    who served South End Irish domestics—

penniless, aged, alone, frayed—
after lives scrubbing and caring for
         other people's homes and children.

Russian bookstores and Korean groceries
now line the avenue over.
         In Brookline's Jewish synagogues

yamukked pilgrims, families chase sabbath dawns
while a mute labyrinth, the Best Western Gardens,
         straddles both worlds.

Death and danger
followed our mother,
         hallowed the nights

like one son's cold blue stare,
his stonewalling tongue's slap
         against pretension.

I've inherited her nightmare:
A stranger stalks me,
         climbs behind

as I mount and mount
St. Elizabeth's steps
         alone.

MONT ST. MICHEL

I.
And must one
be hit three times on the pate,
like St. Ambroise

before taking the hint,
be prodded awake from a deep dream
before claiming old burial rocks

diverting tides that eat the sand,
to make a pilgrim's shrine
to an angel?

II.
I came here first with summer's students
flooding the seaside, transfusions
across countries and cultures in an age
when food was cheap, flights cheaper,
the mantra, "Discover yourself."

My backpack caught and carried seven weeks:
stuffed on a canal barge in Amsterdam,
squeezed in a Hamburg family's BMW boot,
tossed among Boy Scouts on a bus in Zermatt,
in Bruges stroked beside an adoptive uncle,

sun-bleached in Jugland's dunes,
lowered on lorries to Fishguard,
closeted with Edinburgh scholars
and Merton College ghosts.

Love was a commune:
we mixed tongues faster than words
coupled for the price of shared bread,
always thin and sleepy
the world our featherbed,
each city our pillow
every road a journey
just our own.

III
Mounting the hill again,
my steps nudge glint of gold
like that summer's,
windswept grains whisper
along the wide causeway path.

Captained like the archangel,
I rear back my head to heavenly hosts,
hear music, monks chanting,
wrestle to slay dragons like Lucifer
as sea mist fingers the Gulf of Saint Malo,
phrasing the long scroll of my parched way.

Sands surround more than bare rocks.
Before William conquered, he prayed here.
Can I dream three times before I build?

High on the north side's summit,
the Gothic marvel weighs
cloisters chiseled above great halls,
where monks walked and mediated
among pilgrims
and the poor,

an almonry's long list, a bare refectory,
the Hall of Knights, St. George's pledge,
remote from the scriptorium
where near blind monks
copied a dissolving trust.

Hidden below, the cellars,
under fortressed walls,
the slight chatelet
holds on to light and lost poetry.
At the peak, from the slate-torn roof,
the gold Archangel shouts atop slender spires

I, too, would swallow grace's power
trumpet rare music
remember every lesson like a Hildegarde.

IV.

The sea rushes,
soon the mountain
will be under tides:

the dry road cloaked in water,
all travelers left
to an island's hospitality.

CREATIONS BY NATURE IMPERFECT

❧ ❧

(For GAC)
. . . I wanted you to be beautiful
the both of you,
and here among real flowers, fear I failed.
—*John Updike: "To Two of My Characters"*

High above the Pacific north of Malibu,
our steps trail red powdery soil,
loosen stone against stone.

His haystack curly hair, backwards hat, lead,
a bobbing pointer on this geography page
we are memorizing together.

On the path ahead, his tall legs
skirt dry yellow coreopsis,
pace past mustardy sagebrush,

to mount the chaparral-harsh mountain,
rare green an unrequited velvet cover
over its jagged bones.

A young gazelle, his narrow form bolts
fueled on his 16 years, a chocolate bar
from breakfast, and music.

We'd bought no water or food,
only ourselves.

This is so cool,
his voice reverberates
beyond my view.

Below the turquoise ocean churns
waves smash curving white sand coves,
black upended boulders and tittering cliffs.

I trek on, coax glimpses,
an hour into the silent hike
catch up on the iron-flat summit.

He grins, knee-deep in stunted juniper,
swallows oak umbrella shade:
What took you so long?

A forgiving breeze tangles his hair
as Sunday bikers, their thunder echoing below,
cut up the canyon.

Dry as the red dust
coating my pants and hair,
I am ready to rest,

but he points to the road below,
announces: *I'll race you down.*
Just let your body lead.

And we are running,
dancing over cracked earth's snake holes
spinning around curves that edge deep gorges

switched by ghost blooming chamise
fine as rice paper, manzanita's orange bark,
yucca's spikes legion around us,

unlooping the trail down
arid Leo Carrillo State Park
to the sea below.

Hours later,
I am pressed in the middle seat
on the midnight plane East,

his sleep-heavy head
tumbles on to my shoulder.
A Roman nose tinged red glows.

It's a rare connection.

Prickly pears, shrub firs,
houses clinging to
the fragile land we'd hiked,

above fierce ocean, fickle rains,
the shuffle between parent, child,
years already molded:

a dance between humans
and land they could destroy
by loving it too much.

EXCERPTS FROM "LE GARE ST-LAZARE:"
AFTER THE PAINTING BY MANET

ॐ ॐ

Love is . . .
—*1 Corinthians 13: 4-8*

This poem is my gate[6]
to the field behind the fence.

Patience glows,
like Victoire Meurant's beauty,
Manet's odalisque nude
she stares out fully dressed,

---

[6]   Poetry is my gate . . . Jane Hirshfield: *Nine Gates*

gloved fingers mark a place in her book
as smoke shrouds a train,
at station edge she waits
for what is not yet known.

Love gifts *kindly*,
a limp pup nuzzling in her lap,
mist muting this place named for the one
raised from a stone tomb, the fourth day.

It's *neither envious nor boastful*,
resembles swallows returning
to moss-swept archways in old missions
year after year.

Harbors *humbleness*,
fading poppies on Victoire's hat,
exploding strawberry and apple fonds,
cascading curls in rusty gold.

Love has a purity, *nothing arrogant or rude:*
a child's blue sash and white pinafore,
lace at a mother's neck
floating the way fresh snow falls.

It never *insists on its own way,*
but rides in the secret sorrow
between two creatures facing out,
solitary before crowds.

Balancing space,
her posture still,
the girl grasps fence, tilts head,
a nascent body filled by her absorption.

Unposed as a run-away,
love's neither irritable nor resentful,
steady like Victoire's stare, a black ribbon,
pendant earrings on curved ears.

It does not rejoice in the wrong,
unjudging like bold buttons closing
a bodice so often bared for art
in amber candlelight and flickering fire.

It bears all thing, reticent,
two females alone caught between trips
on the corner of Rue d'Amsterdam
and Rue de Londres.

Expectant
the woman's eyes hail the street:
is there a carriage
holding husband, father, painter?

Someone
to steady the journey,
renounce black lines,
open the gate?

Love never ends.

AFTER NERUDA'S "SAVOR"

The inner guitar that is I, keeps the catch of the ballad/spare and sonorous, abiding immobile/like a punctual nutriment, like smoke in the air.

Left behind in the house in the woods
where deer play shadow games
we crafted our own instruments
from spruce and cedar
each vibration a taught string plucked

resounding through bridge and saddle
without ebony or rosewood fingerboards
the nut, a strip of bone
guided the strings
where soundboard met fretboard

we depressed, tight gripped the strings
plucking, strumming
straining the bridge and the saddle
so the saddle sometimes broke
the strings limp on the neck

until
its purpose soldered back,
we took up bare fingers
or a plectrum
to play.

PSALM FOR LESSONS LEARNED AND UNLEARNED

⚘⚘

(March 19, 2003)

Thunderous planes overhead
swollen with ammunition
scream in the still winter night.

We took quiet as our own:
bird song, blowsy clouds
nights mute with infant's sleep.

The buses stop, start in rush hour up 16th Street,
a teen mother clutches a GED en Espagnol
a college student springs from the family shop
a night guard heads home.

Outside my classroom polyglot voices undulate,
men delivered from genocide in Sierra Leone,
women spared soldiers' sly ways in El Salvador,
au pairs and waitresses, hospital orderlies, cab drivers.

Is it bare January branches, ice-chewed ground
that lead my eyes to better see
bouquets of new green leaves and plants
in the summer?

Can we ask to spare from fires and shadows
three sons grown tall as their childhood poplar trees,
to guide them over tests and weighty contents
they've yet to understand.

To comfort in her faith, her sun-bright smile
the ancient mother rising from a cripple's chair
to set the hours and vines growing again
in our spring garden?

Our Father, give us light for windowpanes,
love for those struggling, peace to stench
all beastly bleeding wars,
a lantern for this journey

home.

LAMENT, AFTER PSALMS

Voice harsh,
a rising January wind
whips stiff poplars.
They sway hypnotic
over shadow-riddled ground.

Voice feathery,
sun's last toe dance crosses dusky pine floor
stars emerge from stormy canvas
as painted moon hangs low,
a platter of sliced melon.

I come to speak for a mother
whose eyes are shrunk to black holes
that catch, askance, a face's corners,
sly glance a flower,
the rest blindness.

My mother knelt not once but thrice
to see her own child's flesh
grown crazed and sad, be settled into earth
while she with wispy whitened hair
bones turned liquid by walking years
remains the gardener on an emptying plot.

Now, movement pains
strength leached away as fast as surf on sand,
she todders like some windup doll
behind the walker's bar,
or slowly turns the wheelchair round
to reach a room where she will sit alone.

Hers were always hours full of prayer
a cheek turned, eschewing violence
hard labor for the length of days,
deep benedicted rest come nights.

Oh, yes,
her long dead husband, my dear father
suffering delusions, battled her,
his poet's tongue that shaped roses
turned to vomit and whips when
angry darkness pulled him.

But she bore that albatross
gave the world eight children
fresh flowers, vegetables,
a sweet girl's smile.

Now she sits among cold papers, whispering skeletons
blind, lame, deaf, not wanting to come away
to those who'd listen and keep her precious time,
be beside her when the day is done
to grant this one dear soul her dignity.

Is it justice we measure
in a newborn's wrinkled fist,
in thundering waterfalls in first spring,
in ancient stones and voices, out of Silence?

Honey and Chocolate and the Birth of Sons

Amber dollops of honey you fed me then
Pulse, push, my body opened, to birth that son
Now I harvest spoons from your chocolate jar.

Steady, you urged the labor, fended off fear
Snow walked the seeded fields of Great Meadow
Now I harvest spoons from your chocolate jar.

The midwives' brownstone measured our night's trail
You gave me all the time I needed
Amber dollops of honey you fed me then.

My blood loss large, you found iron pills in an all-night store
Sleepless our child suckled for seven days.
Amber dollops of honey you fed me then.
Now I harvest spoons from your chocolate jar.

Frances Garrett Connell

BALLOON

ᘓ᠕ ᥱᘓ

(August 20, 1957)

Balloon let loose into sky window
   cloud drapes pull shut:
what was round and red and light
   drags itself beyond our eyes.

Up 19 miles, alone
in the pressured gondola,
hanging below the 20-story balloon
Maj. David Simons looks out.

From outside Cosby, Minnesota
in "Man High,"
he's ascended 40-stories
from the Portsmouth mine
to break all records for
balloonists' heights.

An Air Force doctor
he sees stars "in Technicolor,"
they do not twinkle but
produce a steady light, their color—
white, blue, orange, yellow, red—
speaking their age.

In the cooling night
his balloon falls 30,000 feet
rolls in a thunderstorm,
the metal capsule skirting lightning.
Tossing out everything
even batteries, he rides out the turbulence.

By morning, oxygen-deprived,
his speech slurred,
his thinking cloudy;
he lands across the border
in South Dakota.

Weeks afterwards,
Simons tells the press:
The absolute silence of the stratosphere
made me forlornly lonely.

> Outer space soared straight up
> another 12 to 43 miles
>
> waiting as it had a billion years
> for Yuri Gagarin to circle
> the regal green-blue ball
> four years later.

AMBER

❧ ❧

A drop hangs

I rub the pendant's smooth curve
transparent cognac

like no other mineral
it feels warm.

Dark globs jeweled to lighted honey,
track bartered history's trade routes

Washed up along the Balkans,
in Germany, Sicily, England,
in Burma, Mexico, New Jersey

squeezed in petroleum bedrock
as ice crept, flattened
shellacked, embalmed

seeds, leaves, feathers
bees, conifers pines, crustaceans

It's resin mutes horsehair, smooths melodies.
Aromatic, it spills the pine woods.

Unshakable a fly's blood
stays suspended in a frozen air bubble
for 30 million years.

It shines yellow red, green blue,
the purest navy brown a trick of the clouds,
imperfections petrified.

For all its hardness,
warm, it softens,

heat it and it burns,
scratch it and it shows its scars.

Through the smoky champaign brown,
my eyepiece, I see you.

Like swamp air,
press the hot mineral against your throat
to temper speech.

Cup pulsing bees, ferns
stony excretions,
to echo light ambient:

Let tears drop
in hot sorrow.

Last Talks with an Afghan-based
Colleague and Ascetic

☙ ❧

I went to the Tibetan collection, in Newark
straight from Port Authority
a snowy gray morning

Its strange, to re-enter the States in the winter
when people pull in upon themselves
in their insulated solstice,
unreceptive to your separate tale.

Friends? I've few now.
They're elements from a permanently removed past,
your receptacle, your brief Pygmalion:
a friend once left is ever changed.

My lamas from the Dharamsala monastery
journeyed around the world to lecture in Bloomington.
Among Americans, one saw a vast unfocused neutrality,
vulnerability, energy that can be used.

Conversation tends to dilute you,
thoughts uttered often become half-truths.
High from the Flagyl, I've talked too much this year.
Space perception changes
so I think people are moving close.

Are we perhaps like Jung's memoirs,
quite mad but firmly gripping reality?
Are we, working here these years,
propelled by the stuff that pushed
ambulance drivers in the Spanish Civil War?

Sheer magic, that man's mind,
although he missed a lot initially:
motifs, images, always collected,
the import of it all only clear
in recurring patterns years later.

So, have you learned you really want to be solitary?
If you set off to be alone
make sure you really are this time:
don't leave one complication
for another.

Reality is unfetchable.

ON RE-READING *ONE HUNDRED YEARS OF SOLITUDE* IN AN AFGHAN VILLAGE IN 1975

☙ ❧

"Before reaching the final line, however, he had already understood that he would never leave that room, for it was foreseen that the city of mirrors (or mirages) would be wiped out by the wind and exiled from the memory of men at the precise moment when Aureleona Babilonia would finish deciphering the parchments, and that everything written on them was unrepeatable since time immemorial and for ever more, because races condemned to one hundred years of solitude did not have a second opportunity on earth . . . ."

In Macando's
inner-bred generations
among gypsy-teller children

a scholar's esoteric research
subdues generations
to understand his secrets.

Weather itself wanders,
full of butterflies, forgetfulness,
sleeping disease, a beauty's inhuman smells.

The house they live in expands, shrinks
over the century spiders, weeds
inhabit cool mud walls

Rain erases all signs of the modern.
Tortured love, unhealable solitude,
move like light as fragrant planes, clothes,

ideas planted in the dead's memory
waft a century strong, time eternal,
until something moves.

The family's dead return over and over,
flesh and mind
to rule the new generations

until the last Aureliana
taken in by the magic room
Melquiades's secrets,

finds himself, loses himself
deciphering everything put down,
all that was prophesied
in the last lives.

THE BIRDMAN INCLUDES THE BOHEMIAN MUSICIAN

How kindly Lucy Audubon took him in
to the family crypt,
the Bohemian musican Father Heinrich.

Ten years after John,
the *Birds of North America* artist
died in dementia,

she tucked in Anton Philip with her brood
beside Astors, Grinnells, other hoi polloi
in Trinity Cemetery,

up the hill from Minnieland,
where the Audubon farm once sprawled
at the world's edge, and New York City's.

The octogenerian born Krasny Buk, rested briefly:
younger he'd walked the wilderness, 700 miles
across Pennsylvania, along the Ohio to Kentucky

putting down in sound the frontier,
its flora, fauna, native-dwellers
colorful, full-throated like Audubon's birds.

Long since he had eclipsed himself,
pianist, violinist, composer, conducting Beethooven,
founding the New York Philharmonic Society,

touring in Philadelphia, New York, Boston,
England and Germany, outliving contemporaries
to die in abject poverty.

Once, seeking the urbane Tyler's patronage,
he cacophanized the White House sitting room:
gyating arms high as his armpits

legs marching, fingers straining the pianoforte,
he rendered ice breaking on the Niagara River,
the Falls cascading, wind blowing in old growth forests

cannons pounding in war—
until the Executive gently rose
to request a Virginia reel.

Heinrich bolted, bobbing bald pate,
clutching his score
declaiming on Pennsylvania Avenue:

Mien Gott in Himmel, do peeples vot
made Yohn Tyler President, ought to be hung!
He knows no more about music than an oyster.

Like Audubon's silky feathered birds,
his lost pieces unfurl,
complex, expressive, chromatic rambles:

Migration of American Wild Passenger Pigeons,
Pocahantos the Royal Indian Maiden
the Wildwood Troubadoir,

the Wild Wood's Spirit's Chant;
the Dawning of Music in Kentucky,
the Ornithological Combat of Kings,

the Minstrelsy of Nature in the Wilds of North America,
Pushmataha, a Venerable Chief
a concerto grosso about William Penn with the Indians.

His trademark, athematic, stream of conscious forms,
experimental harmonies, whiplash modulations,
modal shifts, palidromes, fantasies on "Yankee Doodle,"

elegies, log cabin dances,
he cannibalized his earlier pieces
touted exile, wise Indian elders, flight,

Shenandoah, Black Thunder,
piles of antlers prayed over on the prairie
before a Blackfood warrior hunting party,

or a valentine to the Philharmonic
which would not play his pieces (and never has),
to them a whir of departing passenger pigeons.

When Tweed, owner of all he could finger,
had his gang run Broadway through Trinity Cemetery,
they silently transported Heinrich's remains one last time

Day laborers, immigrants, moved the bodies
further up the hill from the Hudson,

at the beginning of an avenue
that was never built.

THE SPOUSE'S UNIVERSAL WAIL OF DISCONTENT

But you never heard me,
never valued my separateness
coddled all your family's crazies,
self-righteous religious prudes, over me,

gave the kids all the attention,
spoke of me as a person never present
at their games or recitals or meals,
gave me no pleasure.

Though I remain
a mother's faithful son into her grave
life's too short
to put up with you.

The real world cozies to my language
barbs, hooks, accusations,
squeezed onto elegantly lined pages
sway judges and win cases.

In any city I can eat drink,
pass time with whom, when I choose.
Unlike you, she listens, massages,
makes sex scintillating.

A child yourself
hesitant to take responsibility,
all those years you gave away
your talents, education,

took teaching spots which paid nothing,
insulting me who supported this family,
still supports this family.

I loathe your laziness
the innocent face you give the world,
you who made me an adulterer,

made me abandon all I had worked for
for 30 years,
made me seek comfort and love
on the other side of the continent.

And, while we're listing things,
stop being so stupid,
don't let workmen in an unguarded house,
or forget to lock doors, or mis-add checkbook totals.

And, nothing personal,
those poems you write, refusing to let any judge
scribbled in notebooks you hide away,
well, no one can understand them. Or you.

I get along with everyone
understand everyone's speech,
except yours.

After waiting forever for you
I just gave up.

BY TWO'S

ରୁ ଏହ

Dead people hate the number two
but the number two makes women drop off to sleep.
Frederico Garcia Lorca, "Little Infinite Poem"

Companionship,
completion,
flesh cupping
indentations of another
full womb, coupling, a pair
peas in double rows in a pod,
kindred spirits
doppelgangers, twins

the order of all things
front and back, left and right
north and south, night and day,
yes and no

polarities, poles
what's black, what's white

two parents,
two arms, two legs
two ears, two eyes

life
death.

AFTER WHITMAN

The outstretched wings of a downed hawk
a carooming plane desperate to land
tip from side to side
by Butler Library's picket-saved green lawn.

A weapon-relaying pop, pops, thuds
bolts up eight stories
to lap like flood water
against my red-curtained open window
to drown sleep.

My papers from the home
beside a slumbering creek in another city,
settle into a noisy New York corner room
at peace not measured in cushions.

The cracked stone path to the Red Lighthouse
skirts childhood legends,
humbled by cars and trucks roaring above it
a racing Hudson cemetery at its feet.

Sitting on stone benches along the Park
senors move domino tiles
senoras spin wheels
and call out Bingo.

With sunset the young men
guard the stoops, gather thin-legged girls,
or suck weed on the benches
edging the steep street to the highway.

A tall girl, her legs tucked under,
black snake tresses tangling over her shoulder
willowy green blouse shadowing pointed breasts,
cups her hands, cries silently, on the Subway.

We stop
my eyes touch
the door slams
a child calls.

Frances Garrett Connell

BEFORE CHRISTMAS, 1973

୧୬୰ ୬ଓ

Tashkurghan, Afghanistan

Out the wavy school window
small girls play in a muddy field
I see their hair heightened:
they are all wearing crowns.

In the evening
delicately chewing orange slices
Tom pauses: *"Eating an orange
is like eating someone's house."*

We sit around the tubby *bookerie*
its heat pushes against the mud walls,
snow falls in lean handfuls
in our valley.

Full as old mugs with
nostalgia's waters
we remember Childhood,
other Christmases:

You and five siblings lining a creaky stairs
singing snatches of Christmas carols
for your father's proper Irish lace mother,
as he stares up proudly.

(*"As if showing off pet monkeys,"*
Tom teases,
*"I never knew the words.
They made me mouth them."*)

Self-consciously pious, playing Mary one year
in the Methodist Sunday School pageant,
my Joseph a dimpled eighth grader
my curlered hair unwinding under blue shawl.

When the generator stops, solo lightbulb out,
we sing carols, instruct imaginary orchestras,
sore voices strain to breath old words
into our dark, foreign room.

At the end of the cold gray day
we lay, buried winter logs
under heavy featherbeds
still crooning folksongs out of key,

singing, warming all night
until the mullah's call to prayer
envelops us at dawn:
harmonious.

HAGIA SOPHIA'S MOTHER'S MILK

They are listed precisely
as mundane as a grocery list,
the holy reliquaries protected there,
like Mary's milk.

And how do you preserve it for ten centuries?
Was it daily sanctified
in every nursing mother's donation?

How elegant this trick
among such solidness,
conquerors, conjurers, and ego's
sleight of hands

This place
by divine milk blessed
housed holiness
"in shrines made by eunuch hands."

Emperor Justinian began it,
gathered materials from his empire
stones from Egypt, Thessalyian green marble
black rock from Bosporus, yellow from Syria

to house, deep in it is bowels
a stone from Jesus's tomb, Christ's shroud,
bones of the saints,
and Virgin Mary's milk.

Under forty windowed domes
marble pillars colored like
cool forests and fierce glaciers
reflect gold as fresh as sun-caught rain.

Light bounces everywhere
hovers inside the nave
outlines dome, an umbrella turned inside out
a scallop shell stretched to a parabola of protection.

Light dazzles the marble slates on curving vaults
Christ in sparkling mosaic
golden Archangels Gabriel and Michael
white flowers and birds vibrant in black.

Enthroned above another entrance
the Christ child startles from Mary's lap
as the emperor bows
before Gabriel.

Elsewhere
Christ Pantoculom in dark blue robes,
saints, prophets, church fathers
gospel scenes, the six-winged cherubs
ring the golden ones.

A thousand years Hagia Sophia wore the crown,
this world's largest cathedral,
gave asylum, sheltered wrongdoers,
assembled patriarchs and ceremonies.

Until Suleiman the Magnificent
mounted Islam's golden crescent
arched Mecca with *minibir, mikhrabs*
a loggia to call the faithful to prayer.

Later scions of power hung
giant disks and medallions
inscribed Allah's unspoken, Mohammed's name,
mounted four minarets like burnished swords,

plastered over the Christian mosaics
bells, altars, sacrificial vessels removed
the whole iconstasis hidden under
the passionate geometry of Arabic script

until Attaturk declared it a museum
not a house of faith.

Now intertwined, neither imagery is touchable—
to remove the Arabic calligraphy is to lose it,
to get underneath the Christian mosaics,
is to defy Moslem sacred signs.

Can we call back Isidore of Miletius, the physicist?
The mathematician, Anthemios of Tralis,
whose perfect harmony of numbers and forms
designed the first basilica?

Christian and Moslem squabbled here
over dogma, occasionally some good,

challenged iconoclasts, called idolatrous
gold and silver mosaics, stone by jewel
shaped across the vaults like captured
constellations with human features.

Latin Catholics stormed in the Fourth Century—
neither better nor worse than Suleiman—
they trapped, slaughtered, enslaved
for booty priests, sacraments,

townsmen, would-be refugees,
farmed out all the relics
to their empire,
churches across France and Italy.

Once, a soup kitchen, library,
fountain for ritual ablutions, thrived,
a whole complex served the needy.

But over and over
someone had to shore up the dome,
replace old chandeliers
clean mosaics, remove carpets to show

luminous marble tiles,
the omphalium's decor,
mend leaking copper roofs,
turn rushing ground water away.

Wandering back now
through the iconstasis' web,
that wall of icons and religious paintings
separating nave and sanctuary

you can tilt your head to hear voices rise
from the pulpit where imams mounted stairs
to stand and declare
the sermon.

After they buttressed up the dome
the sky above never fell.

A drop, a vessel,
a pungent smell on an old blanket?

What happened to the mother's milk?

BURNISHED REQUIEM

Granted, they sought innocence
in this family, after their lithe father left
to do his work each morning all their childhood,
returning long past their hours of sleep.

Later to feast on newfound lovers' food
finally to banish himself to solitude
to squirrel away under girth and gin
a spirit so enriched, a mind so keenly sharpened

it began to unroll
like a broken tape recorder
telling us over and over
burnished requiems.

V

The Places None Can Go

AFTER THE EARTHQUAKE IN TALOQUAN, 1998

The stench is different with the women,
no unwashed *shalwar kameez,* stained vests,
oily black hair or Brillo-pad thick beard.

They're flushed, ivory-skinned girls, or
toothless women with wrinkled skin
beyond their few dozen years,
faded in flowery dresses,

green, red, yellow patterned scarves
framing head, neck
under pulled-back burqas, their only shelter.

like tossed away fabric, colored lint,
tiny girls and boys squat randomly
against piles of rubble and mud,
no relatives alive.

The earth spewed, swallowed everything—
livestock, fields, food,
families, livelihoods—

beneath turquoise-shadowed mountains.
heaved, cut deep rugged wounds,
bleed across sheered off plateaus
where fires smolder.

Their dirges rise above prostrate forms,
arms cradle remaining toddlers,
climb into the hills, to restore a past,
to mourn their dead

as the earth keeps raging,
shedding crust,
ominous, no long insulated
truths.

DRINKING FOUNTAIN

ଚ୬ ୯ର

Houston, Texas 1957

I.
Clear wet parasol, the water squirts up
as my child's hand twists on the cold handle.
It heals tongue, coats throat in neutral tones
like sepia dissolving TV station letters
striped black and white bands
signing off at midnight.

Beside me the old man's tongue laps water,
woolly-haired elder made to dip over
metal and porcelain Hinkee-Peelot fountain
like a temple basin.
He bows decorously, left and right,
catches my stare,
looks away.

I count the terrors larger than an old black man:
radio voices reeling off robberies,
children found locked in closets
emerging shriveled up, albino, drooling,
the man who haunts the alley
where friends play Sheepboard Away
huddling in his car, then flipping on his light
to reveal something in his lap.
Sirens aping exploding bombs,
long silent class lines hunched over
hands over head, scuttling under the desks
when the sound pierces,
screaming: the End of the World.

But there is wrong here, I know,
a full-grown man tasting from a tiny drinking fountain
stooping to the level of an 8-year old girl,
above the signs: "White" "Colored"

II.
White is bleach
parts of the skin hidden from the sun
places where ticks can burrow,
ice tipped from aluminum trays
dress gloves squeezed on for a wedding
that will break up in a year,
new underpants and t-shirts
in cellophane packages
anklet socks that go with patent leather,
Sunbeam's spongy bread
you can wad up and coat with margarine,
Easter lilies, insides of melon seeds:
It is the crayon that disappears—
snow, cotton, filled in clouds

"Colored" is a rainbow
rising with mist
after a pelting thunderstorm,
a whole box of paints,
satin reds, sunflower yellows
turquoise morning glories
twining the back fence,
dark cocoa browns—
thick mud shaped into patties
on a make believe table,
clumps of field clinging to a brother's baseball cleats,
moist dark worlds Mother digs in garden rows.

III.
White. Colored. Everything separate
beauty salons, barber shops, lockers for miners
waiting rooms and theaters
schools, libraries, telephone booths
lunch counters, boating and fishing docks
prisons, hospital entrances
reform schools, circus ticket booths
wine and beer stores, parks, burial plots
mental institutes, buses,
public toilets
drinking fountains.

IV.
The man straightens, pats lips with handkerchief
as a woman, finely-netted, lavender hat
nested on head, pressed ivory suit coating slim arm and hip
emerges, grimacing, from the "Colored" toilet.

I nod,
pat newly-permed hair
springing out in ponytails
over jug-handle ears,
hug bandanna midriff,
shorty shorts skimming tanned legs.

In the flooding water I swallow again,
unwinding a pale universe.

PREGNANT WITH E. 62ND STREET

August 1979

In the two-room apartment
two blocks from the river
dust sifted blue grains of sky
out a solo window like curdled milk.

She viewed mornings
from the underskirts of the 59th Street Bridge
a squatting woman:

giraffe-necked, spread-kneed
aching with cab phalanxes
whose shrill honks clawed silence.

After the egg sac dropped
formed yolk into gene-packed man-child,
she wept, water at faucet end
gathered, fell by the hours

public as the neighbor's message machine
beyond paper walls replaying invitations,
or the stooped elder opening cat food tins
on her fire escape across the street.

Coating days with silk smiles,
she paraded her terror in every morning's
marathon on Lexington

melting one day
in a church pew
that granted absolution.

From the world outside her body—
news gnawed into hidden grief—
hostages, ayatollahs, *Apocalypse Now.*

She saluted skull-capped men
corralling sons from *shtel* to *shabbas,*
cocoa-skinned nannies raising a stranger's child.

Undetected she spat at Nixon's brownstone,
hid her swelling under winter cloaks
in Central Park, unbraided milkweed pods,

sent fibers skyward
above model's raw bones and pancake powder finish
past *Daily News* scraps on yellow subway walls.

As the baby grew, and she stayed alone,
over and over it came back to her,
a torpid summer night in Houston:

She was eight, it was May Day.
Dancing the rehearsed dip and glide,
dirdl skirt clinging,
daisy crown pressed down

curls jerked back like taffy pulls
she wove braid after braid
of long silk ribbons
on the school's May pole.

Then the music stopped, no parent claimed her.
Eyes brimming, under smoky magnolias,
drenching oaks,
she walked the dark alley home.

Years past that birth, a blessing,
a rare first son, that apartment and husband
she pondered flight's disguise,
like a second-hand fur's turned-out lining:

satiny, Parisian perfume sweet, but ripped,
another's trash, unwisely worn.

WEIGHT OF A NAME

❧ ❧

(On Giving You Your Great Grandfather's Name as a Middle Name)

It's a lot to set
on your thin shoulders,
this name.

Dr. Alexander Garrett died a decade before I was born,
sixty years before your long legs, whirling arms
destined to cross stages and capture light waves,
entered the world.

His was a family, four brothers named for the famous:
Christopher Columbus, Marion Lafayette, Alexander Stephen,
raised to be lawyers, physicians, business men.

In your own gazing brown eyes
the exploding blond curls
that crisped into black waves
I see their whisper, that intensity.

Out of old albums, he stares
pince-nez a shadow over straight nose,
collar stiff as packing boxes,
he skewers the world with unblinking attention
as if remembering a boyhood surviving

after Sherman burned the swath to the sea
leveled the family's land and livelihood
after his daddy and his wife's-to-be
died in the Civil War.

At 18 he marred Gabriella,
raced through high school
in floundering Campbell County
entered the Medical College of Atlanta, now Emory

migrated by wagon and boat in 1892
to a small town near Fort Worth,
site of the nouveau riche,
railroad barons, ranchers, entrepreneurs
later oil tycoons, just behind the railroads.

The salt to his pepper, festival to his protocol,
your great grandmother Gabriella
loved to read, hated housework
charmed with an Irish wit from her Kidd roots.

Widowed in her final years,
restless at her elder son, the attorney's house
she dismissed their maid one day
claiming no servant was needed, with herself there.

Dr. Garrett's sharpness legendary,
he shocked with pithy words,
a temper like red rose petals pulled apart,
he dismissed the absurd
as quickly as early hand-cranked movies:
a cylinder of light at the back of a
gaping black screen, or scream.

But his heart was generous,
passionate against injustice
he set his own agenda
on issues of health, God and politics

immunized, treated the last native Apaches,
and any poor,
on call at night or dawn
paid in blankets, corn, potatoes, or laundry,

he delivered generations of county children
but lost three of his own eight
to diphtheria, suffocation,
a freak football accident.

See that sternness in the family portrait
the focused steel-blue eyes?
But he shelters my father, their last baby,
in golden girl curls
long white stockings and dress

he tugs his next brother George
hair oiled down, parted in the middle
in suit jacket and cut-off short pants
like you wore in "Chocolat,"

the other siblings already men, women
so much older than he.

Commissioner of Health
tireless practitioner over forty years
Dr. Garrett housed his family
in Palo Pinto, Springfield, then Weatherford
their fat porched house under witch-hat gables,
stood a block from the square,
the county's exact middle,

its sandstone exterior, tall cupolas,
graceful bell tower like something off
Avenue de Richelieu in Paris
the whole place
"elegance unexpected on the edge
of the Texas frontier."

A stage coach factory still stands
from the days before the Santa Fe
when people traveled the Butterfield Stage Line
and the Brazos ran clear and fast.

Millions of peaches grew in orchards
as large as grapefruits,
spring blossoms floated dreams
along with watermelons the size of small cars,
in late summer.

And abandoned cemeteries:
Texans even keep up the dead
through someone else's enterprise.

Old Wild West rodeos and cattle drives
plodded through Parker County
beside Chautauqua lectures and chamber orchestras,
the Baptist fire and brimstone ministers
Dr. Garret disdained.

All the Doctor's children took music, elocution,
prospered in law, business, music,
traveled the world as grown-ups

except my father, the rebel,
who studied French, theology,
then became a clerk
to support eight children of his own.

Imagine them back in Weatherford
on Sundays when the family drove the Model-T
to Mineral Wells, or hopped the train nicknamed
"The Water, More Water, and No Whiskey Railroad"
in this dry Christian enclave,

strolled among watering spots,
multi-layered stone baths,
therapeutic hot springs
where people soaked and socialized.

They took ice tea or ice cream at the café
under the elegant Baker Hotel's shade,
alive then with bands, cattle barons,
Hollywood starlets, military and political leaders

people seeking cures for incurable diseases,
a place now empty except for the orbs,
the dead's spirits, ecto-mists-apparitions—
specters who move random objects
among the dust.

This great grandfather ran for Congress
on the Prohibition Party platform,
ate oatmeal, sorghum molasses, sweet potatoes
unrefined flour, and fruit pies

chortled at organized religion's hypocrites
printed, dispatched by hand his own
anti-smoking brochures and campaign
way before the Surgeon General even existed.

So that "A" initial middling your signature
reflects character, history, rebels worth a pause

and maybe—
when not seeking anonymity
in the film or food world—
your official name with the "Alexander"
spelled out full.

WISHFUL ESCAPES

Someday
I'll live in another house
where gyred winds
nacreous shells
hallow life around me

The dark closets stuffed with
seconds of a now-canceled life—
boxed papers, fliers, table leaves, toys,
tepid clothes, stacked books—
will turn into windows overlooking light

Someday I'll sleep in another bed
lower to the ground than this tossing ship
four mast posts gentled into one headboard
scent of hay and country mornings,
sea spray and wild rose bushes
levitating a lean, aged body
to rest.

LOUISE'S LETTERS

ଔ ଓ

(August 1975)

She penned sad epiphanies
in that cold Montana ghetto,
loved those children
she had borne so mistakenly,
skipped their meals,
to look for money to buy them toys.

She wanted their renegade father
to be liked,
he ham radioed as "Texas"
and "Lady Texas and Her Brood,"
co-signed with "Dead Man."

She moaned about
social workers
"as young as my baby brother"
trooping through the house to investigate
until "Harold ran them off."

Or the woman next door
fighting to ostracize them
in the neighborhood
with traps and loose lips.

Still, a few words smile:
she praised the local cop, a neighbor
with our Daddy's white hair
stentorian voice, short, round stature,

who told her, "Hang in there, Miss,
we're all family,"
when she cried on his shoulder
scented with old cigars

the week before the State removed
her children.

The letter ends
(four more children were born),
ten years later
her life stopped too.

NOTES ON GARDNER'S *GRENDEL*

When the monster tells the story
Beowulf revisited:

silly men play games,
think they think,
but blunder blind, disconnected,

follow *schemes with a vague family resemblance,*
own *no more identity than bridge,*

although they spin, create spiderwebs,
lumber or run,
their facts are nonexistent:

They build the whole world out of teeth
deprived of bodies to chew or be chewed on.

Calibesque, Grendel cowers, fumes.
Terrible violence unravels
in poetic runes:

Alone, of the Great Mead Hall, he loves
the Shaper of the Ballads-History-Spinner.

Single, he must destroy all Danes
who will not understand him.

On Reviewing Old Notes on
Hibernian *Nights*[7]

The fine, rhythmic redundancy of detail
the way all successful adventurers build castles
with a window for each day of the year

the way a wicked stepmother manages to drive
the first born to impossible tasks, fed on a slim diet,
herself home, to watch for his return
from the castle tower.

Or how people on magic journeys or in magic time
always traveled "twice as far as I can tell you
and four times as far as you can tell me
and ten times as far as anyone can tell us."

Or how many stories tell of a person who
sees a leprechaun
do something like shoe a horse
by cutting off the stallion's legs

or cure a king by cutting off his head
or "appear" to bring a person stabbed to death
back to life by whistling at her

then get himself in a fine fix
when the magic doesn't work for him
as it did for the other worldly one.

Just Irish stories.

---

[7]   *Seamus McMahon*

CENTRAL AVE.

❦

You throw out the vignettes
like laughing mynas,
their glistening black wings flapping
the sounds rare:

I see a working class Irish ghetto
in southwest Boston,
your childhood, the 50's and 60's,

yours a street overrun with eccentrics—
elusive 90-year dressed in candle white
stepping in laced-up heels
between snarling bulldogs,

grim poet-philosopher lush
dispersing politics and forecasts
daily walking the street end to end
for brown-bag nips,

the family with a crippled father
who did weaving in the attic
while four sons, three daughters grew
shuttled through Yale, Wellesley and Radcliffe,

the mother
who kept her children home from school
because she feared being alone,

a Polish emigrant, cigar-dripping expression
foreboding revolutionary plots
only a second generation
of quiet undertakers,

a Chinese laundryman, the Hebrew pharmacists,
pickpockets, altar boys, and speedsters,
the police chief's son embezzled art from rich to poor,
locked up, a Houdini, he escaped five times.

Tiny square yards,
limping but roomy white clapboards
mothered every scandal and oddity society bore
then laid them bare, lazy-Susan spun

beside your folk's
respectability and form.

NOTES FROM LAWRENCE DURRELL ON CORFU

෧ඪ ෴

You do best with the olive oil,
its taste older than meat
older than wine,
as old as cold water.

Candles around a saint's shrine
suggest the remnants of human limbs
smoldering in the dimness
before an altar.

A puppeteer describes the landscape:
for resolutions and partings . . .
which precipitate the inward crisis
of lives as yet not fully worked out.

The local recluse, Count D,
calls philosophy doubt
that survives in man like a hookworm
causing pallor and lack of appetite:

one day, awake, a man recalls,
severed from human actions,
his mind irrelevant,
he pauses, lost even before himself.

Reading you in that icy Kabul winter of 1975
when the sun escaped

I heard of words on World War II:
subtropical men,
defeated by a world
where the black compromise is king,

how they were *daily recovering*
by their songs, their poems
the whole defeated world of acts and thoughts
into a small private universe, a Greek universe.

Knowing *there is nothing to be said:*
There is simply patience to be exercised,
patience and endurance
like eternal seas.

A CLASSMATE'S SENSE OF ALZHEIMER'S

You haunt me, Margery
well-bottom black eyes
long ebony curls,
tight intake tummy, narrow child's shoulders

wearing the same ashram linen draw pants
embroidered scallop-necked tunic
ballerina shoes
as during our late 1960's education

still deferring to the speakers
as shy as the 19-years old
who shared the silent rows with me
facing our English professor like an oracle,
in those dark wooden chairs
we noted each pronouncement in wispy script
in notebooks branded with the college name.

I see you and weep
as you tell of learning to love
as you did your toddler children,
a mother with Alzheimer's,
of caring for the mutant, slight body
bringing distractions to make her smile,
her eyes as bright as a Hudson noon.

Terror splatters, a shattered vase
embeds as shards as you tell us calmly:
your mother's daughter
in body and temperament,
you will likely follow one day
with the tangled webs
the protein-ratted amagydia

that choked her memory,
that closed her mind.

THE LAST OF THE ARGON OIL

It bottomed the glass pan
dribbled in to insure an even bake
for onions, kale and potatoes
newly carried from the CSA at Riverside

but I remember it for the goats in Morocco
marble eyes askew,
climbing ragged trees on cliffs
to eat the seeds,
their droppings later collected, washed
the seeds removed, and pressed to make oil.

Sparsely I used it,
drizzled here, there, rare cooking days
in lieu of vegetable oil or butter
spread once on my hands
to heal sun-licked skin

recalling your years in the Moyen Atlas,
your walk-up cement room in Asoka
flies thick as soot, squat toilet, cold water buckets,
silent hikes up the length of the ravine
behind fleeing black clad Berber women
returning to Taliouine

pompous officials strutting for photographs
farmers squatting among trinkets,
the village's rich man throwing out your shoes
so we'd stay for another six courses of Iftar dinner.

Honoring your light-footprint on that earth
you only brought back this hand-labeled bottle
brewed in the battered lean-to women's coop
on the edge of town,

or bought from men sitting beside the highway
selling to passing motorists,
bottles piled high
in the middle of no where.

ON BUSINESS IN GUYANA

The country, a sweating brow,
hangs on like a drowning man
among rivers and creeks
flowing north and east

from the Kamoa and Maccari
tracing tangled jungle borders
with Venezuela, Brazil and Surinam
through unchartered forest,
to the Atlantic.

The mighty Essequibo malingers,
its entrances silted over,
bars blocking Bartica and tributaries.
At its mouth, south, cataracts
channel islands.

It is always the heat, prickling,
a needle-nosed mosquito
drilling pores, drenching fizzled hair
puddling the floor,
an errant child.

A country ghosted,
rancid as greasy rice
plopped beside brown cassava.

Prayer flags ripple like ripped clothes
off balconies, between mud-sodden huts
sprawled over drainage ditches,
in shanty-towns of squatters.

Horse-drawn wagons loaded with junk
skirt collapsing Dutch-English architecture
stained by yellow mold
as if fouled by giant dogs:

long porches, latticed verandas
perch on stilts above
bread-loaf first floors
to catch a breeze
dam a river, stop a sea.

Scions of indentured East Indians
oppose African slaves
touting Old English names
in frenzied annual elections:
a *danse macabre.*

The country a machete
its heat sparks slices.

At the airport outside Georgetown
I sob at the ticket counter:
Find me a seat,
out today, please,

to anywhere else.

PICK-UP

ᘒ ᘓ

(Georgetown, Guyana. January 2005)

The light is kind to me
candles flicker across hotel tables
among travelers

bound at dawn
for the interior.

The man watches
from across the terrace
then moves over

patiently biding his time.
When his lines come,
I know they'll be cliches.

"Can I join you for a drink?
The waiter told me
you were Chinese."

His forehead lucent,
a rat's nest of hair coiled above,
he motions for food.

"A lounge lizard," smirks
the mate of 30 years
continents away,

*"How stupid you were to arrive before dawn,
to plan to leave again in the dark—
with kidnappings, lawlessness rampant."*

This other, in my head, glowers on:
"For Chrissake have the brains
not to get yourself killed."

But the Guyanese speaks in this damp shade:
"Let me study your face
so I'll remember it?"

Later, he sips white wine, fingers grapes:
"I'm bored. Can we just pass the time here?
Two kindred souls, journeying on a doomed star?"

A mile away
the coffee latte Atlantic
laps over muddy flats,

edges the 67-mile sea wall
a narrow gray snake
impenetrable.

Loneliness puffs through the lungs
opens one to listen
just one dark hour.

The airport cab,
ordered for 3 a.m.,
will carry me to a dawn flight
home.

Frances Garrett Connell

NIGHT WORKERS, 1971

ରଚ ଓଡ଼

(after John and Kathy Long's story)

Student-poor, invulnerable
my friend worked nights
in a Berkeley donut shop in the '70s.

Speed freaks with sugar-craving fits
stuttered over sweet monstrosities
bear-claws or powdered sugar cakes.

Timid, slender gays, arm-in-arm,
argued delicately over flavors
closed eyes, pointed coyly
to a pink or purple confection,
and giggled.

Later, waitressing on an all-night shift,
at a pancake house near the striptease block
off the Tallahassee highway
customers sat behind closed blinds and dark glasses,
then staggered out through the pain of sunrise.

In another, not a bar, a hangout for would-be machos
djinns haunted the place in early dawn.
When one customer looked askance
at another's girlfriend,
they tore up the seats
and shattered glass.

One Easter morning, shiny Baptists
in for pancakes after the sunrise service
cracked the dark synagogue of the night people,
sending regulars huddling against the wall.

Her favorite regular—
a stripper—arm crocked in a different man's
always ordered two eggs
sunny-side up:

physique and dress,
busty particulars
mirrored the eggs
she swallowed.

Collecting strangers:
faces, forms,
unfinished sentences
labor while light
fades long.

Frances Garrett Connell

International Conference on Family Law

ഐ ൞

Salt Lake City

Just so we drop
into someone else's universe
learn their language
trace maps of their destinations

Bare this season
the Wasatchs brood
gaunt pinnacles rise to reptilian crests,
their rills the scales.

Inside the hotel meeting rooms
Malayan Shari'a and Dutch judges,
mingle with New Zealand social workers

borrowing Maori faith
to counsel families.
Others debate topics untouchable—
paternity for sperm collected *in fellatio,*

family unity, same-sex marriages,
subtle laws for those spawned
without love
or future.

The scholars vie with conferences for
"The National Numismatic League Collections,"
"Debbie Delectable's All About Me,"
a phalanx of appraisers polished at seizing Western land

I am tabled with
a Norwegian corporate president,
a Maltese Family and Children Minister
and a Swedish lawyer,

the latter recalls a youth
I'd met at Oxford, thirty years before.
Now married, with dazzling sons,
he still invites me to keep company.

Sparse blocks away
at sprawling Temple Square,
the four-spired fortress rises.

Ephemeral white-gowned brides
pose among fountains
dark-suited youth pace in pairs
arms long at their sides
as prairie winds whip skyscraper canyons.

Nail-less, a tabernacle glows under eerie dome roof,
lattices and trusses sculpt arches,
dowels and wedges secure,
plaster filled with horsehair.

In the old Union Railroad Station, murals dance
larger than life above the echoing lobby:
driving the spike at Promontory Summit
to connect transcontinental railroads,

the first Mormon pioneers,
kerchiefed women, long skirts billowing,
men broad-shouldered as gods,
Conestoga wagons tidy with children.
Seagulls flock at a mysterious inland lake.

Below, polished terrazzo floor
transfixed by rose and gold-filtered light,
suggests misplaced ghosts
from the French Second Empire.

A solo violinist leans into his instrument.
Bowing he soothes the western mountains
and all wise monsters,
to play "Amazing Grace."

JAPANESE TRAVELERS VISIT US IN TASHKURGHAN

ର୍ତ୍ତ ୯୭

June 3, 1975

1. Background

Mr. Hawagawa arrives like a refugee
from Genghis Khan
long-haired, Mongol-bearded,
baggy linen peasant pants clinging to old bones,
he carries a rebab, a collection of cloth bags,
over his shoulder.

A writer, musician, an eastern poet and historian
he lives in a small hamlet in Snow Country
high in mountains where the cold white
sleeps year around four meters deep.
Where people sit for hours over their tea,
only the strong-minded venture out.

He explains ancient Japanese speech-style.
a hand-motion shows something—
burial of a word or idea
its emergence from the heart,
from some area above the head,
or behind it.

He'd moved into a wooden slope-roofed house there
among ancient settlement farms,
though people laughed, "Tokyo people can not live in this land."
But later, among cups of tea, gossip
on which neighbor girl should be married next,
people accepted his strangeness.

Losing one house to an avalanche,
he bought another,
houses plentiful then,
where once 60 families lived
only five remain.

For four years
he's raised his own organic rice and potatoes
written, played music
run a free art school for local children
collected his thoughts.

"One farmer, 85, still climbs up his mountain every day
his cheeks polished like hard apples.
His back washboard straight,
he looks after his own rice fields."

Mr Hawagawa glances up to the compound wall
reaches as if to catch a passing firefly,
light accordion folds our village skies.
"My own guests come to see my museum
to hear a concert constructed from my ethnomusicology.

They help to shovel the snow.
Or journalists track me down to do articles
photograph my way-of-life,
but I dislike just being someone's subject matter."

(2)   On Sweets and On Direct Speech

Politely turning down our pie
Mr. Hawagawa explains
how Japanese men scorn sweet things
this sort of food considered women's fare
how amusing he finds European people,
hungrily devouring, craving
cakes and cookies from Kathmandu to Paris.

Then, too, he notes, the differences
in "direct talk languages—"
Chinese, English, German
use a firm "yes" or "no."
But Japanese floats,
full of circumlocutions.

If offered tea or cake,
A Japanese answers something like
"Well, I am thinking about it."
Food must satisfy both his idea of it
and his stomach.
It must suit his whole body
so he stops, lets his body answer
what he "wants."

Crippled with the need for sudden decisions,
A Japanese struggles in a direct talk culture.
Forced into situations demanding open talk
many older men use alcohol
to make them more "social,"
more Western.

(3) On the Old Times

He's seated again and we wait:
"Once the samurai,
the old Japanese warrior, was a hero,
an image people still crave to carry,
the stoic viewing everything from a distance,
his was a head above or behind,
a perfect balance of mind and emotion,
never showing unevenness."

One hundred years ago,
before Meriwether's black steel ships
sailed into the bay
and the Russian boats followed,
the society was stratified,
medieval, stagnant.

Then "Mind" culture moved from the cities—
Kyoto and Edo, to other towns
and modern attitudes evolved
so now even the children in Snow Country
dream of tape cassettes and recorders,
while down the mountain
townspeople dote on cars.

(4) On Food

He tells of his recent weeks in Bangladesh
where food in the cities is scarce,
rice and chickpeas, expensive
available, perhaps twice a week,
how if he got rice and a little potato
he felt honored,
how if an egg came with that
he felt like a thief.

(5) Ideology on plains versus mountain dwellers

"Plains people show more aggressiveness;
those in flat places
must cultivate sharp, forward movements,
while those in hills or mountains
move with a circular mildness
up and down, around,
a motion that lends itself to
more peacefulness."

The second night he sang and played
the *Rubi' at of Omar Khayyam* in Japanese,
the words gruff, low and haunting,
the Persian reconciling
ancient Eastern cultures,
once trade partners.

"What does it mean?" I interrupt
when he reads another one,
his syllables howling low as a scratchy wind.
Mr. Hawagawa smiles:
"The poet cautions
people who makes things of the sand

to handle it with great reverence,
mindful of objects shaped from it,
of water put in it,
for the sand is the fine dust
of beautiful girls long dead."

Later that night, our guest stretched in a worn sack
in the narrow two-room mud house,
I hear his voice singing rapidly
in Japanese, released.

5.   *The Tea Ceremony*

Preparing to leave the last morning,
he gifts us with a tea master's fan
carried all the way from Japan
for this moment.
"Do you know the tea ceremony?"

It takes place in a small house, in a yard,
the structure made of paper walls
so natural light pours in.
Against one wall, a simple flower
artistically arranged, as incense wafts,
its scents drifting for hours.

One by one, one follows the stages,
the turning of the cup
the heating of the water in a small fire
the putting in of the powdered tea,
the presentation of the cup on the fan
with a full bow.

Taking it from the tea master,
the guest turns it to him, to his heart,
sips, tests the cup for its pure sound
gaging the master's good taste and skill.
He says a few words on the tea,
renders thanks,
completes the ceremony

For centuries suitors also used the ceremony
to test a marriageable woman,
if she understood such protocol with grace
she could succeed in giving her partner
a harmonious, and charmed life.

He stares at me, glances down discreetly,
bows his head, under the long draping hair
a small willow tilted slightly:
"But you know there are always answers,
the simple deepest ones, if you listen."

He tells us of a wise man a hundred years ago
who performed a tea ceremony for a king.
The royal sire came to his town after hearing
of the wealth of flowers growing there.
The tea master had all the flowers cut down,
then arranged a single branch in his tea room.
When the king, greedy for a lot of everything,
saw the starkness in the village, he raged.

"But his lessons was before him:
that one pure sample of anything
is all one needs."

RED-EYE: THE PICTURE NEVER TAKEN

The sun teases all skin gold
all eyes electric, their father's face unlined,
three sons grin with gelattos

even the baby stares, as we glide through
cobblestones in ancient Lombardy
between museums, churches and huge lunches

returning every night to the Nesso villa
I've rented from the old professor
its narrow uneven steps, unwinding to Lake Como.

We never catch his pose
eyes flat, limbs frozen
on the balcony above water plowed by ferries

his wine poured into small crystal bowls
anger sheeting the huge bed of his discontent
as he sips in the sharp, silent day,

I scrub out two weeks of dirty clothes
in the cold water bathtub
tread hot steps and unlearned Italian

to get soda for a child with a traveler's bug
I bless sunshine, ocher-dazzled walls,
three active sons.

Frances Garrett Connell

Hating my ingratitude,
I weep myself to sleep
under Capricorn and Sagittarius

splitting round checks with a smile
my eyes, sunburned for sure,
edged in red.

VI

OLD SOULS

FROM MIRCEA ELIADE'S *SHAMANISM*

In Yakut initiations,
each shaman's Bird of Prey Mother
shows itself at the shaman's birth and death:

*"It takes our soul
to the underworld, leaves it to ripen
on a branch of a pitch pine."*

The magicians move in caves and labyrinths
between doors that open briefly
only for the initiate,

remain open until
the aspirants bear out their dreams,
meet helping spirits:

Always, if the journey is to continue
we must deny proffered food
ignore the semi-divine woman

glimpse and withdraw from the dead
climb the tree, the mountain peak, the ladder
while the eagle soars, bird of the sun.

In every place to know the language of animals,
especially birds, is to know the secrets of nature,
which lets you prophesy.

In Central Asia, Altaic shaman
descend to an Underworld like Dante's
to a *place where sinners are tormented:*

one man who listened at doors in his lifetime
is now nailed to a port by one ear;
another, who had slandered, hangs by the tongue.

Here upturned pots,
broken pottery before graves
confirm the underworld,
for Altaians, Gardi, Yuan Central
and North American tribes
since anything inverted on earth settles normal
among the dead.

Like the Turko-Tatars,
can we imagine the sky as a tent
the Milky Way as the seam
the stars as the holes for light,

our eyes divine lanterns
to a world twirled into lace?

APOSTLE'S NAMES

Strange? A coincidence? Some subtle flashing light?
Or only a season for naming male children
for parents' childhood-learned religion?

But my Irish Catholic
faith-abandoned husband's sons
all Celtic-named,
raised among free Methodists,
early chose best friends for life named,
like New Testament books,
Mathew, Mark, Luke, and John.

And which inhaled the wild-eyed mystic,
the Word's origin,
a gospel unlike all his brothers',
narrating neither exits nor entrances
only tales of a Holy Spirit
giving everyone
everything?

On Memory and Sweets, April 2011

୧୨ ୧୨

1.
I was the child, bending bottom up
duckling on dry land
to fetch the fallen candy by the road,
furtive, fingers fierce and quick,
I tasted it,
sweet and full.

Raised in a house where I'd
read late nights on the bathroom floor
facing scurrying roaches who'd
declared our fecund house their home,
I'd creep there to avoid Daddy's fiery welt
words condemning my light pouring
under the threshold to his bedroom
from my room.
There was nothing to fear in bugs' wanderings.
Their scattered bits visible and invisible
in kitchen drawer, cabinets, ceiling cracks.

We'd eaten it all and survived.

2.
She worried we were the only women left
under her piny promenade, after my husband left
and—bow tie askance, spectacles askew,
asleep after his regular 6 a.m. walk up the street
like stretched suspenders—
her bold old chemistry professor one passed on.

"We'll have to meet for dinner one night," she cooed
her Georgia twang as ripe as July peaches,
the curving crown of her dyed brown waves dancing
above the fold-down collars from her 40's college days.
"Yes," I'd promise," winding down the tarred driveway
after the 60 mile commute to Arlington, or Baltimore
these jobs with social workers and health educators,
stunned refugees and endangered immigrants
I'd taken up to earn my living.

The years came,
yellow and red falls, poplar and oak shedding,
springs' dancing redbud, azaleas, dogwood
winters sheeted in snow, summers cooked like rare meat.
I worked, she called, we never met for dinner.

Then her heart stopped, she was buried.
I missed even that, my post card penned
from a foreign land,
still caught in her bundled mail,
inky words wishing her well
running in the April rain
like my undeserving tears.

MEMORY AND FORGETTING[8]

ରେ ୧ର

Let out now
the paper spirits
Chinese magicians kept shut up
in closed books

For it is the work of memory
to throw out what is not our own
to select a simple line, a scene
deliver it to the visionary mind
transform all

We yearn for resolution
like the tale of the "The Black Bull of Norroway"
or Drabble's "The Waterfall:"
One a woman visiting her lover
who lies in a coma in the hospital,
the other a serving girl
addressing an enchanted knight.
Each sings to the loved one,
recalling all she has done for the other,
beseeching him to "wake and turn to me."

No one's memory is whole,
there are separate ones
for body, feeling, mind,
conscious and subconscious memories

---

[8]   After *PARABOLA*: "Memory and Forgetting."

Like Jala al-Din Rumi, we can chant:
"For sixty years I have been forgetful every minute
but not for a second has this flowing toward me
the unknowing, the source of all knowing
stopped or slowed."

Belief and doubt,
two sides of the same mind
worth only as an exchange of knowledge.
If crystallized, opinions, they gain us nothing
But, questions, they gift, lead us to ask:
"What then is certain?"

In fact,
not fancy,
new knowledge flares.

Frances Garrett Connell

REPATRIATION CASES 2004-00712
AND 2004-00971

ை ⁀ை

When a person returns to his country, the leaves of all the trees he stood under in foreign lands change color and fall down, and one by one, the mad ghosts of every betrayal circle like cinders sucked upward in raucous songs.
-Old Frances Adage, source unknown

Red is the color of poppy petals
pregnant with bulbs and seeds
this spring day.

Raven-headed her curls
once tangled over shoulders
sharp as razored Pyrenees.
She cooed back the Spanish sun
tongue ullalling
under sea-scent pages of
Neck Ring of the Dove.

Madras dress
flared inches from the dusty sandaled
feet she'd pilgrimmed on
following him below Grenada
to stay.

One link in her chain of days
snaps, not fetter-free,
she savors
tooth-like imprints on her wrist.

Women, men
going home
among ornaments of the world
broken bodies.

      ***

Now she floats:
below, Mediterranean sea sleeve
un-braids white gray threads
beyond the plump peninsula
where years had held her sewn.

A second woman beaches
above the Mediterranean,
cross-straited acropolis
on light-bleached cliffs
mimic clogged birth canals

Young as persimmon sheen
she'd fled Chicago's winter knives
to make this, a Majorcan lover's,
her home.

On a forested hill above St. Luis
her final days pulse
measured in lassoed ferries
clotting rough sea to Barcelona

Skeletons claw cliffs,
along dagger-sharpened rocks,
into the horizon she swings
wrestling Olympiad girth:
young men left on painted pot shard,
her own breath tinny as broken glass.

***

Which one had met in *dhimmi's* shadow
frail as four centuries' syncretism
gazing above a bridled northern sea
one Oxford winter

reading the begging bowl tale
prisoners secure in medieval towers
sketching a nun's retreat
sanctuary in founded college stones?

Which traced the harbor to Moorish Spain
Jews, Christians, Moslems flowered as one
before the salt rubs of the earth?
Back below Grenada a fat widow sighs.

The women, their skin lose with the years
pause, countryless:
the angle of repose, Stegner called it
a formed perspective

like *mihrab* prayer niche in horseshoe arches
arch after arch mirroring where phantom
whirling dervishes spun skirt
in Cordoba and Seville.

Held in their palaces of memory
patinas of reds, ocher, the Alhambra,
rusting as the village well water
now plugged up

or in the tiara white cake painted villages
their single monument
chapel, mosque, synagogue
each onion-domed.

It is not easy to bring them home
after their thirty years away,
put one in a Florida residence
monitor her depression
keep knives and razors far away
until she finds the means to live again.

Let the other's life be structured
by a Massachusetts brother
away from the foreign spouse turned abuser
back in the hard safety of a new state.

There were *fatwas*, troubles aplenty
and hagiographies
a cleristy, in this time of Al-Andlus
among Rome's spolia

chanting the ring songs
the *muwashshaha's*
rhythms encircle,
repeat, link stanza to stanza
Scheherazade's stories
mirroring one the other.

In Toledo one mounted the hilltops
and the framed tale:
Ibn Khaldun's *Mugaddimah*
Chaucer's visit.
Out of Saint Iago, Moor-killer's story,
archived reliquaries spoke tongues.

Here the visible, invisible, dangled, evoked
palatine cities, Don Quixote manuscript.
Here cradled mother tongues, Castillian,
langue d'or

The names march between their legs
like rapiers
each violated by their infidelity
why couldn't peace remain
or the past?

Kilometers from the village
where that one-time lover died
left her destitute and mad at 56
Here Bopubdill relinquished keys
to Isabelle and Ferdinand.

History bled forth a *hamra*—
Red.
Red.
The walking dead.
Returning.

NEWS OF GRAND-MAMA'S DEATH

ᏯᎲᏣ ᏣᎲ

Kabul Afghanistan, July 25, 1973

Tonight you hold me, grandmama
in this country where we have no roots
in bamboo shaded light,

as two lithe musicians
stroke drums and rebabs
into the sounds of earth,
somewhere outside these mud walls.

I see your webbed face
gentle girl's eyes
telling your Francheska goodbye
out of your dozing 87 years

that last day home
a German primer's blessing
in your thin, almond whispered voice
our lifetimes joined in a forbidden kiss.

Light and soft as a child doll
you were easy for Him to lift away
your Deutsch courage
back scattering feathers

in a Brenham farmyard
that buried motion,
all my childhood dissolving
in Texas dust.

As your days had been,
in this country, people bending,
laboring constantly

on sun-burnt earth
their soiled lifeline daily wears
musty from unaired rooms
the outhouse's limy stench.

The blessed break of heat in night.
the brief morning grace,
remind me of Texas summers

when, free, a child
I wandered amid
the foreign wonders of your home
while Grandpapa, the stern man, watched.

You, too, kept crumbling cookies
under folded rags
in old glass jars,
plucked limp chickens,

christened our thirst
with garden watermelons,
offered us your mineral water
from the well

cut stern home-backed crusts
and strong dark coffee (Texas tea),
for our gnawed, rotund stomaches,
excused us for our craving for soda pop—
in the face of it all.

At night at your farm
the dogs barked,
their generations stalking the barnyard

the light bulbs hung naked
with giant story shadows puddling
around themselves
and we listened into morning.

We are apart now
that time and place lost,
inside me only,
outside our common face.

The news reaches us three weeks
after your passing,
we sat in remote Gardez,
in a teacher's house,
when you closed your eyes.

Beyond us now
we pull a string for a magic garden
come as close as the midnight door
when the whole world shifts.

Our grip slips, reality foggy,
our craving thoughts can't bridge
the gap between them.

Yet we nurse our strings,
questions on the brim of tears,
as the sun shines.

Between the worlds, the words,
she has moved away:
to a peace

for all we travelers.

GRANDMOTHER ASHORN'S FUNERAL

ᏩᏴ ᏭᏎ

July 1973

The day before she died,
Uncle Herbert flew in,
country boy in ill-fitting new suit
his first plane flight in 60 years,
he stayed at the boarding gate at Lambert Field
because he didn't know where he should go.

At the funeral
Charley Brown and Fanny's six-foot-five
twin sons dwarfed us as pallbearers,
Charley was Great Aunt Ella's only son.
Pretty brunette cousin Margie
editor of her law review
Holyoke degree behind her
working that summer' in Washington,
read the 23rd Psalm,
while her mother, Aunt Lillian, glowed,
sorted out cattle shares and fresh salads to feed us.

Uncle Walter in raggedy hat and suit
drove a dented car, the day off from teaching History
in Eagle Pass near the Mexican border,
shoving his mild little wife, the nurse,
nondescript in a bun hat.

A whiskered, blue-eyed neighbor farmer,
wizened and sun-scrubbed like the Grandpa
who died when I was four,
mother's doddering aunts,
Czech-speeching cousins, a whole clan,
patted all strangers' shoulders:
we had never met.

They carried her hallowed-out shell
suited out in the lacquered box—
this woman who'd worn hand-me-downs,
her oldest son's discarded shoes—
to the old cemetery outside Brenham
a damp, unseasonably cool Texas day
intoned prayers, tossed flowers,
then planted her under a tree
against a wall beside Grandpapa.

Back in his Houston apartment
pacing in his bathrobe,
downing M&M's and chocolate milk,
big brother James, wifeless, wept—

for the farm, our fierce grandparents,
ancient childhood summers and weekends

the funerals to come.

AGE

And
what happens to the old ladies
their hair turned into butterfly wings
pale powder puffed over pastel veins
bird-sharp blades
poking up from their backs

after the razed cradles
hour glass meals
tucked in spouses
when the children have grown into people
who cut deep troughs in the ground

where creatures who crawl need no prodding
cleared out swathes of memory
quickly as lye seeps
replaced discolored sections with threads?

Who remembers then,
these were the ones
who bought for themselves last?

Sun splinters drive into their sagging chests
caves as cobwebbed as high attics
the crags of their marooned faces
erode into marks
in sub-alpine meadows
their thoughts flash
light as thrashed straw:

melodramatic, a frieze leans
heavily on the back
of their waiting room chairs
where once they dealt in strength
bend over now to parody and fear.

Who cares now
they are only a bundle of
their collective words
a list of regenerative hips
macular diseased eyes
arthritic knees and trembles

pious old ladies praying back
their hearts
massaged by the intern's exam
their lover long since gone,
modest and blushing in their
gapping gowns?

LESSONS FOR THE POST-SEPARATION
BEDDED ONE

We housed the rooms to last,
solid mahogany bedroom sets
children's pine bunks and desks
we cushioned each board with silk cloth.

No bodies remain to steady them
grind their shape,
like leaves, they've puffed away
left bare, unwoven threads.

This bed now I sleep on,
linen stretched,
softness turned to stone.

For 30 years
we curled here,
neurotic, I had to touch you
to sleep.

The river reflects black,
admonishes the lesson
you can talk yourself
to rest:

First, wear the body out
run it mile after mile
without feeding,

so shards worked daily
into skin, eyes, mind
recoil, stop cutting
as the stomach gnaws.

Second, read past midnight
until eyes blur
cram words in

like ancient silver coins
weighing sewn pockets
or Yap stone money
too heavy to move.

Third, weep from every orifice
eyes, nose, wrist, breast
so sodden husks un-peel
leave only your dry form.

Fourth, terrify your youngest son
a Daedalus plunged from Icarus's chariot
from brothers, devoted mother, doting dad

so he avoids your eyes
entombs himself behind
a slammed door
drowns the walls in jarring music.

Fifth, travel, so the unfamiliar
tingles and drives,
mesas swallow skylight

rivers tangle, forests move
unknown languages cloak you in clouds
while no one has to know your story.

Last,
collect adages,
write epitaphs,

compose poems.

Being a Nanny in Flavigny During the Filming of "Chocolat"

❧ ☙

(for Erin and Mariana)

The story takes place only in this town
yet its scenes crisscross worlds
beyond the plane tree-lined canals,
chateaus and fecund wine cellars
past cattle fields, the roads
to Haute Roche or Menetreux.

If you follow the path out of the Potern Gate
past village well, glance at the Calvary,
the settling rock
they call the Pat of Butter,
you can wind
through dense meadows and woods

cross a road, take another,
to enter the Ozerain.
I remember like mist
the gray streaks rose across my moon face
as beyond the river plunged
beneath bridges of the Morzain

skirting Vezelay, Semur,
round towered, medieval ghosted hamlets
while dancers skipped
on cobblestones in Flavigny's courtyard
like flowers cascading
out of mildewed walls.

Smoke and mirrors
sharp lenses, turnings
carved out a story whose youngest actors
we'd been brought to tend,
this neither our stardom,
nor our writing.

Yet in the pause of a butterfly's wing
your child-woman's opal eyes
taught us to move among people
collect petals, wings blown loose
from each floating story
and your own.

A breath's perch
on the stalk of golden *azul* plant
in Burgundy's new May
we touched
mist, dust, wind
to light
as film.

PIEIRIDES, PLEIADES AND SISTERHOOD

*Many a night I saw the Pleiades rising thro' the hallow Shades
Glitter like a swarm of firefiles and tangled in a silver braid . . .*
                    Tennyson; "Lockley Hall"

We've got the whole cluster covered.

To start, the Pierides cockily adored their own voices
so challenged the Muses on Mount Helison to perform,
then doubted the judgement.

Victory-less, cursed to transform,
they were changed into magpies,
creatures with unstinting power
to chatter and scold.

Over and over
Greek order cried for maiden's blood:
Hyacinthides, the Spartan princesses
sacrificed in Athens

to appease plague, earthquake,
Minos' vengeance,
although only Athen's capitulation
finally stopped catastrophes.

Sometimes the maidens acted first:
the king's daughters pledged to die together,
after Otionia was to be sacrificed for Eleusinian victory,
so he lost them all.

The Pleiades, river maidens of Pleion and Atlas,
chased in Boetian countryside seven years,
changed into doves, astro-morphisized among the stars
with the rogue Orion panting still behind them.

187

Thousands in that open cluster,
on winter nights, the bluish nebulosal embraces
starlight scatterings, minute interstellar dust
plowing through hydrogen gas.

Always the brightest, Alyson,
the halcyon hen, still days of wintry solstice,
a queen, she warded off evil,
survived Poseidon and seduction.

Beside her twinkling Asterope, the lightning,
sun-faced and stubborn-orbed,
Aries ravished her; later she mated
in happier marriages, and mothered three sons.

Celaeno, swarthy, conceived sons by Poseidon.
Electra, amber, alloyed with silver and gold.
Maia, the most beautiful, Zeus seduced,
to become Hermes' mother.

She named the blossoming month of May,
modeled grandmother, mother, nurse, great one.
Number six, Merope, a mortal, the elegant bee-eater,
married long-suffering Sisyphus, and stayed obscured

Finally the long-necked Taggele,
also seduced, also a bearer,
another who propagated
the pre-Greek race

each thrown up to heavens,
once sister the victim
of stronger strangers
claiming divinity.

ONE HOUR OF CVS REALITIES
BEYOND STONE EFFIGIES

What good are these lyrics about crypts
a frozen wife and husband
stone effigies, a pair who in life
had arbitrated distance?

I see a different picture
flesh-tested, the CVS clerk, Muebla
his Sudanese history burned into his arms
scars, pox-like marks
in the un-braided leg tendons
at home, a family imprisoned
a noose awaiting him
if he returns.

Or the Filipino clerk, Jose
inducted from his village
forced to soldier at 18 on Macau
his shot arm amputated.
His sister, Maria, suffered a stroke
when news came:
another of their brothers, Jesus,
rebels tortured to death.

Frances Garrett Connell

Or the Sri Lankan cabdriver
who waits as I pick up the medicine.
Trained as a chemist, he escaped death
after the Tamil Tigers labeled him a collaborator
in the Land of the Buddhist Tooth
where war turned people to stones for 28 years.

You send something about effigies
stone coffin carvings?

But what of these dealt death,
then a pound of flesh seized?
What of breathing people
shattered like bone
still in this life?

IVAN THE TERRIBLE

When Ivan had their tibula snapped
down-turned heel's fine line cords
threads taut as silk cummerbunds,

when he cauterized the ringlet rose
a small burnt finger's print,
then conflagrated the entire family—
pregnant daughter, son-in-law, brother,

when he had each Tartary head
lined up by size of eyes,
gluttonous tissue dripping from impaled skulls

on St. Basil's turnip-corbeled domes
(whose creators, legend tells, he had killed
so they'd never create another edifice more beautiful),

when the greased skin petals
peeled from stark wired bone,
nails cupped in enameled brooches,

to avenge Novogorod,
expand the Czardom,
quell gossip about disloyalty,

when he threw out the last loyal *boyars*
to be mauled, limb by limb
torn apart by dogs,

faces shredded to cabbage,
garroted his own son and heir in a fury,
his rod's sting opening his skull to death,

history seared him as "terrible," "inspiring fear,"
measured his harm by bedeviled graves,
by public tantrums.

But when a man and woman,
unseen, soundless,
gnaw at each other, rip up faith

hammer words into empty mazes,
claw flesh,
eviscerate hearts,

we call them
only common.

ANGER'S ON-GOING DRAFT

❦

Strained lines wipe out numbers,
mourn open gaps
as his thin pencil seizes
the final sentence,
to gnaw out illusions.

A curdled rain
drop by drop under torn leaves
he makes brittle prose.
Wind catches
in the wounds of his words.

Without ink,
he glazes with his own blood.
There's no other story to tell:

in the end, his could fit
in a common Kleenix box.

"Among the Quadi, on the River Oien"

೦ಌ ೮ಌ

*Words that everyone once used are now obsolete, and so are the men whose
names were once on everyone's lips: . . . . For all things fade away, become
the stuff of legend, and are soon buried in oblivion . . . . So what is left worth
living for? This alone: justice in thought, goodness in action, speech that cannot
deceive, and a disposition glad of whatever comes, welcoming it as necessary, as
familiar, as flowing from the same source and fountain as yourself*
(*Meditations*, Marcus Aurelius,
IV. 33, trans. Scot and David Hicks)

It is 166 AD.

On the edges of Empire
this silent man
foreign to his own home,
stoic among strangers

scrawls out his thoughts
late into the night
on this,
another mindless campaign
to secure Rome's borders

from Germanic tribes
in the heartland of future Moravia
western Slovakia, lower Austria.

In the shadows the invaders
taunt his sleep
whole legions armed
to rush his minions.

In his commander's tent,
the flame burns dark
singeing his own mortality
sorting out the precious
from the dross.

Awake, each cell tingling,
his mind a bonfire
in the cave of his fear
he pens:
What is this state,
and why don't I live like this always?

Aurelius knows the cold sips
of the brook by his villa
the evensong of piled clouds
weaving above his bee-sung orchards
the taste of fresh bread.

He lives out his father's modesty, his mother's simplicity
her aversion to the "ways of the rich."
He loves philosophy, and justice.

These returning armies will carry a plague:
pandemic measles or smallpox,
will slay five million,
including his co-ruler,

then put to sleep himself,
the last of Rome's good emperors.

MOTHER HEARS THE TAPE OF REVELATIONS

*But it says in there, Book 21 I think
"there will be a new earth and a new heaven,"
all our tears will be dried.
But all that other stuff?
I never understood that book.
Has it all happened already?*

Did it already happen
(like blood on the bed, a son's suicide
iron-ripping train, a daughter gone,
heart-stopping sadness, a third child dead,
her own dark tunnel to blindness,
pain and immobility, her 90-year old bones)?

She winces,
pulling in her left leg,
a forgotten angle
perched on the black wheel chair
eyes glowing under soft, elegant wrinkles,

*Angels, and demons,
deep pits and pestilence, destruction—
what could it mean-and
all those different seals to be broken?
And the Lamb knows the final tablet,
and it claims he can unseal it?*

Eyes blink but the face is gentle
like a small child's.
She starts, the sun pouring over her
I glimpse the dry words
held still as a bud
one day from opening.

We speak of the seven cities
exiled John wrote to from Patmos
Laodicea's rich wool and curing ointments,
little Philadelphia's open doors to the East,
faithful Thyatira's fine dyed cloth,
Sardis's gold mines, hill fortress,
Pergamum idol worshippers and tall acropolis,

Ephesus among temples, libraries, history
reclaiming its first love,
while Smyrna the emperor's pride,
queen of the traders, overflows
in wine, garments, perfume and gold.

"Asia Minor"
we giggle at the phrase
port cities, rolling hills, all Turkey now
so unlike Asia Major.
(Is it like Ursula Minor and Ursula Major,
the great bear or one of the dippers?)

I fast forward the tape,
know the line is somewhere.
Revelations 21, also Isaiah, she hums.
I skip around,
past the seven pestilence-laden seals,
the ultimate earthly battle,

past the lions, calves and eagles,
the sun turning black,
past red dragon, the throne, the horsemen,
people all prone to starvation, wars, chaos,
the marked and unmarked,
trumpets, and small edible scrolls.

The moment passes.
I bring her chai tea and Fig Newtons.
Under the sun's umbrella
earphones falling out,
she slips off her shoes,
and sleeps.

40TH EARTH DAY (APRIL 22, 2010)

On earth day
my toes cleave clay valleys,
calcified roots
yellow as tobacco teeth
bend, claw.

Under thin-veiled stockings
pressed tight
in second hand mules
I trip a runner's crusty sole,

they lead along the muddied creek
where Carolina bluebells
blurred violet umbrellas,
reach up to dogwood blooms:

bleached sacrificial paws,
bloody imprint
cornering new leaves.

Frances Garrett Connell

DRUNKEN SQUIRRELS

୭୬ ୬୭

The squirrels are drunk
  sated with ivory dogwood berries
   off-violet velanium,

they pound and roll across the roof,
   their stretched tympanum between the gables,

flip gray curved hides from laurel and fir limbs
   race in quads and covets

   until the acorns
   rain and crackle.

SPEAK UP

Acorns split
oak's waking mouth
sputters,
words held back
jettison.

Like the Polish woman's
furrows
lines left
by folded wings,
her thin shoulders
suppressing laughter.

A DISSERTATION ON MOONLIGHT

*(Preened from a lunar ludic
who observes all
from a rock-hanging house
above Kabul in May 1976)*

The waning moon
fills us with certain excess energy
none can attune himself
to such intensity

I remember as a child
waking up, my head in the window
moonlight flooding my sweaty brown hair,
terrified I would become insane
for sleeping in that light.

I perch here now,
enclosed in turning skyscape
a full moon clamors from dark clouds
a beacon in the ocean:
sleepless,
sane.

PASSING THE PEACE

ᏆᏧ ᏫᏯ

This cathedral
a rich song the steel mogul
built on the Hudson River bluff
to honor Gothic architecture
and his Presbyterian mother
steadies full this morning.

We say these words
turning widely from our velvet-cushioned pews
under luminous faces
from frozen parables and patriarchs
as sunlight punctuates with rose and blue fingers
the shroud of our privacy.

We say
"The Peace of Christ be with you,"
taking each word,
a white stone from our mouths
setting it down for a neighbor
picking up their damp, bright stone
touching lightly with extended hands
a small pat,

as strangers wait around us
like hungry birds.

Frances Garrett Connell

WISDOM FROM VERY SCATTERED
JAPANESE POEMS

∽ ∾

Lady Kara's tanka
was written for Yokamachi:

To love a man without return
Is to offer a prayer
To the devil's background
In a huge temple.

A Muromachi Ballads says:
Men's hearts, like the nets
of Katila's fishermen
are best drawn in the night . . .

In the light of the day
men's eyes
are everywhere
watching.

Or Tachibano Akimi's *Poems of Solitary Delight:*
What a delight it is
when skimming through the pages
of a book, I discover
a man written of there
who is just like me . . .

What a delight it is
when everyone admits
it is a very difficult book
and I understand it
with no trouble at all.

NATIVE AMERICAN MEDICINE WHEELS
AND GLOBAL WARMING

1.
To the old Plains' chief
all creatures in the universe,
except for stifled Man,
naturally harmonize with their surroundings,

which makes Man lonely.

So beyond the four quadrants,
humans spend time alleviating loneliness
creating a new dimension.

2.
In his culture, people grow
into their names.

3.
The Medicine Wheel:
cyclical, like all things in nature,
claims directions.

North is white, wisdom,
green, South innocence and trust,
East, yellow, illumination;
West, black, introspection.

Each has, as well,
an animal, keeper of elements:
Earth north, the buffalo;
west, Water, the bear;
Air, the eagle, east
south, Fire, the mouse.

4.
Scalded, burned dry,
today, I only see the mice-eyed people:
myopic, scanning details without scope,
they scurry daily through finite lives,
as the great wheel spins off course.

ON MISSING BROTHER JOHN'S WEDDING

❧ ☙

December 23, 1973,
the night decades and deeds ago,
John married in a Nebraska town.

On the last train's ragged stretch from St. Louis
trestles swathed in snow, roads dressed in white
Mother and Dad traveled
to stay with the bride's parents on their farm.

I imagine
a trillion stars like docile diamonds
sparking creations or its illusion
staring above,

see them all asleep
under mountainous home-hewn quilts
tatted by the bride's Swedish grandmothers
while outside the business of winter's sting
went on.

I wonder
what the local Lutheran pastor said
as they exchanged golden loops around fingers,
what music bowed and sawed
before John and Kathleen left for their Ozark lodge.

In a land and time fraught with damners of visionaries
what private ecstasy was theirs?
Had they tamed the chameleon iconoclast, my brother,
or only suited him in new clothes?

And, among them, our youngest brother Dan
eighteen under a mane of hair
in Mid-America's narrow pomp
dreaming a complement in notes
watching it all, the skeptical artist.

And Mother,
who'd picked up John from hospitals over and over,
tried to cure with attention and love,
the deep welts in his brain, the chemicals akimbo,

knowing his reason's fragility
could she hope?

Or stormy, bitter Daddy, in his
white-crowned seven decades
did he wear his fear as a dry-cleaned suit,
did he flourish in the sociability?

And John?

Three weeks after the event
I read of the preparations
six thousand miles away,
in a country seven centuries behind them.

Nor today,
all parties dead but Dan and me,
the country I was living in at war,
can I see those cold lost festivities
without weeping.

ROPEMAKER, GERMANY 1973

☙ ❧

Overnight in Frankfurt
our overloaded suitcase popped
we need to find rope.

Down Brouibackstrasse and Damstrasse
beyond Munichstrasse's combat zones
we follow to a square past round Romanesque cathedral,
guild halls' mannered figurines
carved into stone,

to a shop
pungent as a stable's harnesses,
bulging with cut twine and hemp

A long scarfed,
sandaled couple enters,
looking for raffia mats,

a secretarial assistant breezes in,
rabid for twine,
a police woman,
the "Sheriff of Frankfurt,"
checks in with a wave.

The full-faced owner cuts hemp rope,
thick as a python,
then, conspiratorial, he winks:

Those so-called cowboys in your Wild West?
Did they really use those lassos well?
He circles the rope and swings it
ready to capture a bronco.

Little lass, you know,
I sowed seeds first, in my time,
traveled, smoked hashish in Algeria.

Walked the length of Spain,
dived off of Thailand, a paradise.

Once he watched a Maori tribe do a rain dance
then offered tobacco to the chief, who stood up tall

to say in impeccable German
This is all fine, but please speak German, I'm Pokko's son,
He was a German-trained leader,
and I studied there.

When he shakes his head sadly, we look back and nod:
These wars and armies? Having armies to keep peace?
It's like giving a boy a drum,
then telling him to be quiet and sleep.

He mourns the maimed, the killed in every country,
hates American bases, applauds anti-war protests,

chagrined at Frankfurt's "little Chicago" atmosphere,
how gangs and derelicts, *by nature robbers*
learned quickly *from their American cousins.*

Modestly we stand beyond his counter
until in mock horror, he starts,
stares down at my feet:

A mouse has made a hole in your sock.
Now use these scissors to make a twin
in the other sock, so they match.

Hearing we're on route to teach in Afghanistan,
he smiles wryly:
Broad shoulders, a strong back—
you will carry the load of many people.

Then, knotting our burden expertly,
shaking our hands in his large honest paw,
he calls *"Auf Wedersehn.*

This strong length of rope
for you is free."

THREE FRIENDS OF WINTER

1.   Bamboo

In November
our neighbor, the rarely there Dr. Patterson,
wielded a Brit's notion of ownership.

He brought in sun-stolen day laborers,
to scythe and saw away decade-old bamboo,
curtaining the silent woods between our yards

The nightmares raged
our household tossed off horrors—
dagger-clutching rapists swarming the bedrooms,
stomach-clenching footsteps portending thieves,
swollen corpses bobbing in the creek at hill's foot,

here, and in the stolen Himalayan nation,
family woke under wool blankets sweating, worried,
wrapped in miasmas
facing chimeras bold as our eyes.

2.   Pine

They had planted the trees
when this sterling son was born
Their only child, called home now,
he pivots the car out of the street,
under the tall pines
as gentle as candyland sentinels.

He pauses, moves onto the porch,
peers in at the hallway, still lit up
ten months after his mother's passing
as his daughter,
doctorate in genetic husbandry in Iowa,
his son, head of the chemistry lab
at his grandfather's Michigan alma mater
carry in a single suitcase.

Longevity
green foliage, pines,
a season's death,
the cold.

3. Plum

To fine-brushed Japanese painters
out mastering their Ming and Qing coaches,
as they orchestrated long harmonious scrolls
for monasteries and shoguns,
the fragile blossoms evoked
nobility, refinement
precursors of spring.

But in this neighborhood
where trees divide, creek lingers,
whose first house-builders
one by one now curl into themselves
each in his last seasons,

the first hints of purple
spark life.

THE WILD PARROTS UNDER THE 159TH STREET AQUEDUCT

They squawk, unseemly,
jarring, the rhythm exotic
scattering their lime green—
blueberry-threaded—
feathers

quaker parakeets,
they hunker in the bare cherry tree
five days after Christmas
as the Hudson swirls and shimmers
across the New Jersey palisades

the leader hoots down at me
apple-seed eyes peering over hornbeak,
forehead shiny as a pressed gray suit
echoed in cheeks, throat and chest,
out to delicate white-tipped wings

they swirl in sync, calypso dancers,
scatter and re-form
under the murky green iron girders
where their twig and vine nest
hangs elaborate

free-standing, communal:
they share
with other species and birds.

If the nest becomes too crowded,
that season's young females
simply don't mate.

DIRECTIONS FOR SURVIVAL

ⓒᴅ⌁ꞓᴅ

If your dog digs a hole, fill it up before you leave,
the Dog Run Rules tell you,
along with removing him if he starts a fight,
cleaning up behind his droppings,
in field and sidewalk.

Simple dictates for any life,
leaving the ground the way you found it
not gorging out trip-holes for the next comers,
tidying up the waste to leave clean space

not raising rampaging soldiers
but disarming them until they calm down
so others can bask in the sun,
retrieve sticks
chase each other in friendly circles
in unadulterated peace.

VII

TRAVEL THEN AND NOW

GREECE AND TURKEY, 1974

LEAVING KABUL FOR ISTANBUL

July 18, 1974

Kabul only an ancient dream
turned rueful:
the dry appetite that swallowed us
13 months before
now watered.

Five hours beyond the
brown deserts,
Istanbul springs,
gem domed, frescoed mosques,
latticed minarets and red tiled roofs
crowning hillsides above
azure Black Sea.

Black-scarved women
weave around snow-headed
apple-checked elders
sleek young Turks twirl dark hair,
eyes keen, features chiseled
like classical statues

We stroll cobbled streets
where Islam's sounds crystallize:
a covered head, clean feet,
sweet tea, strong coffee,
a bold voiced call.

BUICKS AND STUDEBAKERS

❧ ❦

(Entering Istanbul 1974)

A cold water slap,
a metropolis again.

At the airport we haggle
for a bargain cab,
then whirl into a mad freeway
lined with 1950's American cars.

Big-finned and humble-fendered
Buicks and Studebakers
shined up and purring virginally,
they clutter the road.

Our driver races to brake, pivots to miss
a car stopped in the middle of our lane,
raises an arm to swipe the air,
shrieks wheels as the car moves on.

Veering, we enter the Byzantine city gates
climb up a cluttered hill to Sultan Ahmet.

Outside the mosque, set up like game pieces
goblets, turned-up silver slippers arrayed in rows,
set us wondering
what land we've reached.

ISTANBUL: A DAY ON THE ISLANDS

ଐ ୧ଓ

(July 1974)

After days of losing ourselves
in narrow, steep-winding sidewalks
unnamed cobblestone streets,
the Sea our single certainty

we ferry between Aldoiwi, the Prince Islands,
four vegetative gems in the Marmossa
old resorts climbing the eastern sides
velvet, green blue sea swirling below
like a dancer's skirt.

At the final island
we eye the wooden houses
like carved chess pieces,
gardens cardinal red with century acacias,

follow horse-drawn surreys
carrying cool-faced visitors,
the drivers a cross between
Irish tinkers and Italian gigolos.

At island's crest gingerbread turreted houses
shadow palm trees and flowering birches
between squares where people sit and sip
beside pinecone-needled lanes.

Later, swimming, we own the sea,
until, inhaling fresh fish, fetched and fried,
we dine off the wharf
from a boat moored with a gull.

ISTANBUL: SANTA SOPHIA

൭ ൫

(July 1974),

From our narrow Sultan Ahmet hostel room
across from Santa Sophia,
we pause, then enter,
bare-footed before delicate piety.

Byzantine frescoes, bold arches stare back like ghosts,
in this strangely empty shell of power and Christianity
left by its conversion to a mosque by Ahmed II
decades before Columbus.

Pacing expansively carved mahogany galleries,
past bare walls, I think of an elegant old train station
now poorly kept,
then look to floor and find the miracle:

intricate mazed mosaics, ebony and ivory,
still vibrant below.

TOPKAPI SARAYI

Five centuries
Sultan's glory and decadence
perched on the promontory
over the Bosporus and Golden Horn

Now the old kitchen
collects Chinese porcelain
Ming blues like theories
of ocean, sky and clouds
set to stone.

In the Treasury
emeralds, diamonds
the size of fists and feet
adorn crests, turbans, swords, tea cups,
ivory and silk cover golden thrones,
even a horse's headdress dazzles with pearls.

In a sanctuary of delicate domed tiles
the relics of the Prophet rest,
beside another room
airy with elegant scripted scrolls,
rose-blue Persian miniatures.

Finally the labyrinthine heart
four hundred rooms rich:
in this harem the sultan housed
two official wives, 200 concubines,
eunuch from Africa,
and himself.

Running water sounds
over ornate tiles and marble
where bearded sultans lounged
on plush velvet embroiderd cushions
while diamond and gold-set fireplaces,
and palace spies,
glowed warily.

CROSSING INTO GREECE

July 20, 1974

In Alexandropolis
we find a city perched
on the edge of war,
a national alert
sounds an ultimatum to Turkey
calls every man from 20 to 40
into the army.

Seeking a route to Samantraki
for hours we wander the streets
sit at the train station
waiting for a train that comes
only to take soldiers,

watch truckloads of
rural men carted in
off jobs, farms, fishing boats,
the restaurants missing
their young waiters,
at a pen's drop told
to ready for war,

families parting, pausing,
not knowing: *Is war imminent,
already raging, only rumored?*

By night, a steady beat:
clanging tanks, armored cars,
troop carriers pelting asphalt,
spreading out khaki green,

while olive branches slip off
new inductees' glaze-eyed brows
as they sit in antique tanks,
waving.

The only music
armed men marching
wives, mothers, girlfriends
weeping in tight gatherings
listening in the breezy night
for some truth.

By morning we find tickets out,
elbow through mobs,
for a seat to Thessaloníki
push back against
the bull-dog-faced woman
who raises her lardy form
to knock off a third.

Then, we are moving, seven hours,
Kamotini and Xanthe
detouring up the mountain to Drome,
down again to the coast
in a cloudburst,

evacuated over a rickety bridge
as the radio drones
a dark tongued Greek Orthodox mass.

The dutiful bus conductor moves
up and down, circling a stairwell,
raising, then lowering windows
for fidgety women,
taking down packages,
emptying a dripping light
cheerful as a character in a children's book
he touts company valor and humor.

A mass chanting exile
permeates the air,
as army trucks,
covered with olive-branches
and the young
pass us nonstop across the road.

In the land's pine-covered hills,
black-robed, tall-hatted priests,
lanky black-skirted, scarved matrons
moved among white-washed houses
under round red-slated roofs.

The mass ends,
none goes in peace
except the hills, perhaps,
dotted already
with soldier's pup tents.

Sturdy, wild,
they have weathered
more violent centuries
than any of the
present perplexed
among them.

First Impressions of the Greeks

ௐ ௐ

In broad strokes, we catch them:

generous and head strong
given to explosive shows
of anger or joy,
big and frequent eaters
who will pull you bodily out of your seat
then turn to offer
their *loukoumathes* or *kataifi,*
dusting you with the powdered sugar

Large, aquiline-nosed
thick, curly dark-headed men,
soft, slightly down-turned eyes
capable of arrogance
or flirtation,

women, delicate as dolls
solid as washerwomen
dressed black as the evening strolls,
or crystal in Parisian mini-skirts and necklines.

They kid and tease each other non-stop,
seem docile.
are desperately independent.

All generalities
of pine-clad, cypress-studded land
where olive groves sustain—

sea skimmed,
separate.

FIRST TIME ON THE ACROPOLIS

꧁ ꧂

July 24, 1974

All morning
this free July day

we move into marble temples,
gracefully perched Athena Nike
commanding a virgin's view
of Victory's temple,
the world below,

enter through the Prophylacea,
follow the ramp for sacrificial animals
to studded antiquities:
fragmented columns, truncated statues
smoothly worn marble slabs
connecting the Eretreum's
delicate maiden porch,

to the Parthenon itself,
white brilliance, rhythmic colonnades,
scattered rhythmic friezes:
mythical animals, solid matrons
stately athletes, pontificating philosophers,
magnetic, mysterious pieces
of a 1200-year old jigsaw puzzle.

Frances Garrett Connell

Winding back
through cool cypress shade
down rocky, olive gnarled hill
past graves,
we direct the sun

to enact fantasies
in the theater ruins of Dionysus.

THE MILITARY FALLS

ᕰᕲ ᕘᕲ

Athens, July 23, 1975

In the gathering dusk
eyes brighter than rising stars
we climb above Athens
to stare out.

Loud honking,
voices shouting, a flooding crowd,
announce the junta's fall after seven years:
Ionnides' resignation, Papadopoulos's fall,
a country's return to civilian rule.

The young race by foot, by car
in loud, twentieth century chariots,
chant and wave flags
through tangled Pleka's streets
around Akropolis Hill

"It is over.
Censorship, the EAT/ESA torture.
Remember the Polytechnic martyrs.
Throw out the Praetorian Guards! "

Older residents pour from stuffy clinging houses,
clutching shoes, a hat,
among steeply winding neighborhoods
gather at corners to look at papers,
quiz local, black-robed priests, each other.

Startled, we wonder, wander down,
to a garden where ancient pedestal stands
offer footstools to foreigners,
a family of orange tiger cats
huddle silently as a witches' coven.

In a lantern-lighted courtyard
under arching olive trees and grape vines
we eat cheese, salad and lamb
until retsina dizzies us to softness.

Shadowed,
we sit in another sidewalk cafe
on Parliament Square, watching,
imbibing the free night.

Moving toward midnight
students march on the main avenues
for the new Greece:
we wait like chess pieces to be moved.

ON SEEING SOPHOCLE'S *ELECTRA*
AFTER THE JUNTA FELL

ༀ ༀ

In the Herod Atticus theater
beneath the Acropolis
the shadow lights lift themselves
through Roman archways
where dark-robed actors and actress move,
the chorus wraps around
the petulant first daughter
like a heavy wind.

It is a play about a man, a family
already ancient history
to the Athenian audience
who first saw it in 380 A.D.

In a first century theater built
by a Hellenist-loving Roman
this night, this century
an international audience pauses
as the attending Greeks
cheer the theme:
youth overcoming tyranny
a new order replacing the corrupted old.

When Electra finds her brother alive,
his identity revealed,
the amphitheater explodes,
screaming, "Z! Z!" "He lives!"

SUNSET FROM PYNIX HILL

ରୁ ୦

Long sleepy shadows straddle the hills
swallow the large orange disk
suddenly, regularly,
a drunk imbibing his jug.
Then, gently, it's night.

We find a garden
butterfly cool and shadowy
a nook beyond the lively streets
to eat and listen to the classical *laiko*,
the stroked *bouzouki*, a country's secrets:

sad and beckoning
like toned sea breezes one moment
turned into shouting, sung sin another.

Pausing before Some Pieces at the National Museum in Athens

⤲ ⤳

In a carved grave slab,
Hermes leads a young girl
to the underworld,
the eyes turn liquid
away from her earth people.

Aphrodite threatens a goat-footed Pan
with her sandal
while Cupid hovers over their shoulders
in a humorous Roman effigy.

Bold and mellow, the head of Antikithoria,
the philosopher, studies our world,
where a jockey melded to a steed
spurs on the racing horse in the wind.

A young man's sculpted face,
perfectly formed, malleable,
his tight curling hair,
noted tendril by tendril
on one side,

the other half
an old man's countenance, turning,
transformed, face lined,
eyes squinting, crown bald.

AGORA

❧ ❧

The old Agora scatters ruins
court buildings, residences
Thereseus' well-preserved
temple to Hephaestus

small and dark beside
expansive pyramidal leanings,
delicately fingered sticks
of a roof in praise of Athena
further up the hill.

But don't you want a child?
the tall, black-haired husband
of three years, bends into her.

The Greater Athens Stoa
huge, reconstructed,
houses pickings and choosings
from the yards around.

Look at their daily life,
she motions, continues.
*So similar to ours. Still, there's
no more security in the world today.*

Pottery evolving
up to the perfect
black glazes of Pericles' century,
articles for graves,
jury voting, citizen elections,

the *ostrachia*, a child's potty,
humorous sketches on urns
cooking utensils, cups, pots
a grill and portable stove.

Forget it then, he shrugs,
If you want eternal assurances
that we'll never have.

They stop, touch lightly,
beside beheaded statuary,
small torsos time has left behind.

ATHENS CATHEDRAL

ɶ ɷ

On route to the Teresium
we pause in the gilded
Byzantine Cathedral
where pilgrims pass
from shrine to tiny shrine

Bent crones in black stockings,
dresses and scarves
tread the floor stiffly,
concentrate bright and mobile eyes
on the icon before them,
their ritual cant a few tottering steps
to the next station of the cross.

Blue and rose, silver and gold archways
rise from paneled wings,
the altar a separate covenant,
Old Testament style,
preserves a sadly dignified face:
radiating mysterious pleasure.

"Come, come,"
a voice belts out of blackness,
"Take in the blessing,
pray for all mankind."

But we keep walking through
the dense wooden door
beyond candlelight and incense,
into the searing Greek sun,

free falling from
the discipline of prayer.

On Route to Patmos

ରେ ଏହି

(July 1974)

The boat floats us smoothly
across waters
between shadowy stark islands
bathed in mist
into clear green sea,
the sunset's crescent yolk
suspended above fortress-like land
the night all stars.

Face-up on the deck
atop our sleeping bags
we echo the dark company of spirits
who glide across decks
of glistening ships
watching the heavens
from beneath a cool wind
dreaming of constellations.

On the boat with us,
400 Greek inductees
just called up to fight
the lost regimes' s war in Cyprus
spin us stories,
tip dark cold coffee
from dented canteens,
as we drift under Venus and Mars.

PATMOS DAY ONE

❧ ❧

Did they all come
by sea-splitting, foam-frothing ship
over jeweled water
to this tiny Aegean island
bathed in peace?

The dark medieval monastery
crowns the tallest hills
where black-capped bearded monks
move silently through cool cloisters,
chapels, aloof to this century.

Behind heavy carved doors
gold and silver halos hold up
doleful saints and martyrs
wane Christs, Mother Marys
etched on slabs of wood.

Below Chora's winding stairs,
steep narrow streets
hovers a barren coast studded with caves
like missing teeth,
crystal water

reaching into infinity,
square white houses
one-room, domed churches
clustered as sun-washed villages
hugging the hills.

How is it here,
St John's fiery visions
galvanized exile, fueled
expectations of other comings,
through two rancid millenniums of fear?

WALKING UP THE SPINE OF PATMOS

We walk the spine of Patmos
past Kombus, onto Lambis Bay,
red tiled roofs like leveling wet hugs
smooth blue and purple pebbles
courting our shoes.

Out the valley of stone-walled farmer's fields,
up the long road above
bellyaching blue water
two midgets in a sleeping giant's
magnified landscape

we climb toward sunset
into pure white St. Christophos
clasping the rocks
where dawn masses stiffen the faithful.

Now a table of capped men
argue in the taverna
across the shaded street
beyond a bend in the sea,
where the Hermitage nestles,

in another bay,
some ancient sea captain
whitewashes his walls
like fresh ice cream.

By night the pudgy village cook
dances from table to table
giving orders and free baklava,
offering fresh goat cheese.

We sit among Greek families,
tourists: a golden bearded man,
his chattering son, quiet daughter, silent wife,
a newly wedded couple
drawling with Alabama,

a soft-faced Austrian,
her curly russet-headed friend
quick as a Welsh boxer,
a matron, motioning beside
a dark 20-year old, her son.

Like us,
two John the Baptist-maned teens
rest time-lapsed eyes
on water.

RHODOS

❧ ❧

We watch the island come toward us
like a well-dressed lady
graceful stags edging tiny harbor
beckoning the old Fortress and Lighthouse of St Nicholas
a trinity of windmills slowly turning arms,

beyond church spires, untended mosque,
silent balconied houses
where medieval Christians,
Greeks and Moslems
rubbed damasked shoulders.

Unchanged the old city unwinds
its narrow cobblestone lanes
garden courtyards, iron grilled windows
steady among minarets,
tiny shops tucked away in crannies.

In high noon lanes
the Palace of the Grand Masters
center for St John
of the Knights of Jerusalem's Hospitalier,
spins out its massive turreted estate:

mosaic floors, strong wood inlaid curlings
wide echoing chambers
recall Crusaders plotting
behind moist candle-flickered
stone walls.

Among museum archways
Aphrodite washed away by sea water
nods at a Rodin nymph emerging from stone,
a daughter telling her dead mother goodbye
tilts toward a pentameter of women
astride lions, holding their tails like sceptres,

they balance a futuristic siren's leering looks,
radiant beside funereal urns
on which a lyre player, a sculptor,
horsemen, and maidens bowed in prayer,
move delicately through black and orange glazes.

By dusk, at the old harbor
the Sound and Light show
explodes in the Palace gardens:

It is too brash, too light,
too dramatized, too modern.
We search the sky for stars.

BIKING TO LINDOS

❧ ❧

(on the Island of Rhodos)

Slowly, painfully, we pedal
up a slippery bowl's sides
out of the city, up two bare peaks
the slopes of Mt. Strongylos,
then down-curve, free ride.

In Archeangelos, our half-way point
a gossipy narrow-streeted town
stretching from Archangel Michael's campanile
around arches and walls with ceramic plates,
we inhale fresh bread baking in wood-fired ovens,

join the locals at the central cafe
where an old women nods
at our sweaty forms
in late morning's glare.

A hundred motor scooters pass
as we dawdle, straining on gearless bikes
as lame as the small wild black horses
once used for threshing grain.

In Malon, porches of grapes
turn yellow in the sun
beyond the first mountain,
families in small basket trucks
gather olives.

Six hours later, scarlet and sore
we reach Lindos, rent a room,
pause at the faint mark of the cross
etched in soot on our door
from last Easter's candlelight pilgrim,

welcome showers like a thunderstorm
as the cobalt blue Lindos eye
to ward off evil spirits,
stares from the pine-planked wall.

Protected by a medieval Christian fortress
the ruined acropolis perches above sheer cliffs
lapping topaz water,
beside the quiet bay where
St. Paul sought refuge in 58 AD.

In the still wordless air
tavernas tune for late night songs
patrons gather to sip ouzo and *tetsina*
under gothic, Byzantine Greek,
Syrian doorways and arches,
dip under carved facades and windows,
tap feet over black and white
chochlaki pebbled floors.

Out our window that night,
a parade of flickering candles winds
up the rising road to iconed chambers
in the Church of Our Virgin
soft light burning
among the dreaming pious.

When the bus refuses our bikes
the next dawn, we pedal out again
up the two sinister mountains,
down past small villages,
roadside tavernas,
Archeangelos's staring citizens

puff, red-faced,
over sneaky hills
to the long glide
into Rhodos.

THE ALTA WAY

ᏣᏍ ᏗᏍ

(Rhodes, July 1974)

1.
In a valley riddled with waterfalls
old wooden bridges, the butterflies flock
to Liquides Orientales trees
the pure incense-like sap manna
to multitudes of fluttering rainbows,
Panaxia, of the species
Quadripuntaria Poda

Landed on the backs of leaves,
they resemble black and white medieval shields
a million flash across the cool vale
bright red-orange and black,
more numerous than fall leaves
in a November storm,
they come here to reproduce.

Stomach-less,
the males can not eat
until they mate,
the females starve
until they lay their eggs,
each glides with energy
stored as caterpillars.

The road winds back into Theologos,
a village solely supported
by the neighbor's secret winged population.

2.
Down a wooded hill
past Komiro's bare plain,
then up again, Rhodes' oldest city,
lays mostly under water
a remnant amphitheater stretches
on wooded slopes high above the sea
before Prophet Elias' ominous mountain.

A stillness lays across
the sleeping town's foundation
destroyed in sudden earthquakes
over and over.

Up the road
at an olive wood factory
an old man turns the lathe
to form a chalice,
around him candle holders,
made from groves
cultured on this island
for 3,000 years.

DRAMA IN A RHODESIAN THEATER

cɤ~ ↄɞ

In the moon-bathed hillside
four millenniums old
a crippled arm of the temple rises gauntly
among mute ruins,
dim crumbling pathways.

In the stadium, shadows beyond us,
loop olive groves, oleander bushes
and hard frozen stones to
the audience gathering before the stage.

A boy of five folded between
two broad German ladies sings,
"It's a small world after all,"
then crows: *"I know when the play will start."*

Sighting the long procession of robed players
coming down from the bowl
of the stadium, he hesitates,
"These are not really ancient men, maman?
Just men in ancient clothes, right?"

His twin unwinds from the mothers,
wakes when the ghostly blinded Oedipus
rushes out of the palace.
"Is he going to die now and end the play?"
he stage whispers.

Eerie, gorgeous,
the gaunt-faced chorus sways,
lean-lined in dull purple robes
they shout up to the god as the dirge begins
vowels mellifluous, echo gathered darkness:

small-statured, bull-voiced Oedipus
saintly, cold blue-eyed Tiresias
a harlot beauty of a Clytemnestra,
the comic elder messenger
the pawn of fate, old Sheepherder
weep, exhort Sophocles's terse tongue,

as we sit hugging the cold
drowned in the swirling tragedy
unbound around us.

More Rhodos

Out early, we walk to the Odeon
the Temple of Apollo Pythias.
From partly shaded worn seats
we imagine players in the Stadium.
The wind pushes across the mountainside
eroding sandstone and marble shrines.

At Ilyios massive lukewarm waves
embrace us, dreams in a liquid sleep.
In the old town at a taverna,
by a crumbling mosque
we watch the lights reflect across undulating roofs
while locals roar with Greek songs,
enticing us to follow their drunken revelry.

At the medieval theater
a windmill's shadow moves across bare walls.
In a small square behind, lighted archways
fill up with agile stepping dancers
as the orchestra drums, fiddles,
spins clarinet, plucks *zulieka*.

At sunset
we discover another island
between ourselves and the sun:
at the last minute
this land swallows the golden ball
voraciously.

SKYPHOS

They tell a story about the cup,
the skyphos

how, during Anthesteria,
Athen's holiday to honor Dionysus

to celebrate wine's maturity
from the previous vintage

social order is turned on its heads
slaves join in festivities,
the dead freely roam the city

everyone has his own goblert
to drink from.

This practice, legend says,
goes back to the time

when Orestes, a matricide,
arrived in Athens.

None wanted to share a cup with him
nor offend him either,

so each person took his own drinking vessel
to go to the temple and celebrate.

So the custom continues.

IRAKLION

ல் ல

For over a millennium,
the five-foot tall Minoans
ruled the sea-trade peacefully,
fetched canvas ships to, from
Egypt and Asia Minor

their craftsman and architects
built many-storied modern apartments
several stories high with roof gardens,
carved out staircases with sun well lighting
installed plumbing and drains,

made theaters and artisan workshops
magazines where they stored
oils, grains, wine
in six foot jars.
dug labyrinthine foundation rooms,

sculpted alabaster thrones for palaces
with central courtyards, marble and stone colonnades
circling rounded steps where people sat,
for dancing, meeting, ceremonies, awards,
the bull-vaulting,

fearless and pious before their gods
they filled ritual basins with lustral water
created long processional entrances,
with sacrificial pillars
consecrated by star and a double ax,

In the bones of Gnossos parade full murals:
their sleek bodied, long-lashed youths,
bejeweled women in topless bikini dresses,
follow rapturous after holy acrobats,
leaping their sacred bulls.

CRETE

ଗ୬ ଏ๛

Across the hills
cloudy green olive groves
cross Messara's Plains
lacing together
villages tucked above
the Mountains of Idi.

At Gortyz, an odeon, tables of laws
define the duties of man to man
in a zigzag Cretan dialect
while Phaetos' legends
unfold under hills
in intense sunlight.

Malata's blue beaches,
caves and carved Roman tombs
bedded hippies and nudists one season,
bone to bone,
while around Malia's fertile valley
and the Lassinthe plains

where water flows
from octopus-armed windmills
patches of bananas sprout
among the ancient carob
trees that grow at 1,000 meters
folk saviors who thrive without sustenance

Here, early people carved pillars
from meteors fallen millenniums before,
worshiped in natural mountain retreats
along glowing coasts
where coves fall
as deep as velvet tunnels.

Up in Krista's mountain church
under ancient light, sallow miens
long limbed, large hands and eyes
define Byzantine frescoes, the Macedonian
iconic round faces cloaked in cinemacolor
all stern saints shouldering

Gournia's many basined
two-story houses,
light wells and cascading staircases,
rise from ancient prints of paved lanes
among fragrant thyme bushes.

Along the Cretan coast
the peaceful waters pray
at each cliff foot
behind battering mountains
each island heart
dissolving in gray haze.

Chiseled villages,
even white walls
curved red tile roof
declare a mad roof maker's
benediction cap.

THE JEWEL MAKERS

൭ᴎ ๏ᴄ๏

1.   Early Minoan Crete

Even 4000 years ago
in your small, clan settlements
you loved your jewelry
bedecked your women

you made things of copper
imported precious metals
from Sinai mines and Nubia:
hairpins and chains
diadems and necklaces
tiny animal figurines with
long tapered clutching fingers,

set rock crystal, amethyst
pate de verre,
redstone

in long silver filigrees
you traded with Sifnos in the Cyclades
or shaped into daggers,

carved nautical shapes, bodies, animals
botanical scenes
on bone, ivory and precious stone.

Your potters sculpted
large chalices, sprouted goblets
round-bottomed jugs and teapots

the dark clay
painted violet and white
in simple spirals and lines

and you buried your dead in thalos tombs
simple beehive vaults
cut in the hills.

2.   Minoans 2000 BC

When your central authorities shaped
the palaces at Phaetes, Knossos and Malia,
they structured elegance
storerooms and craft shops
ritual chambers and royal chambers

on the Phaeto disc, frail child of clay
figures run spirally on both sides
children, men, women, fish, insects
branches, bows, ships,
still secret in its mellow hieroglyphic,
perhaps a hymn celebrating
the same creation and life we have.

Like your potters
painted in whites and reds
on dark brooding earth
ornamented with flowers
stylized people on jars,
teapots, cups, on
egg and fruit stands

or the meticulously-shaped
clay and bronze figurines for worshipers
dresses free lined, hair styles elaborate,
the delicate seals in agate and jasper
someone's private symbol
finely chiseled into tiny cylindrical stone

along with famous gold work—
ornaments in child-rich fantasy shapes:
animals, birds, sea-creatures,
griffins and sphinxes
along with statuettes,
gold, ivory and bronze human forms,

a pendant of two bees
on either side of a honeycomb
with a drop below it
recalls Zeus, first son of Rhea and Cronus,
born here in a cave at Mt. Idris
raised in secret from his father
on goat's milk and the honey of two bees.

Traders from their island kingdom
like your predecessors,
you courted goods
from Egypt, Syria, Cyprus,
the Cyclades, Kythera
presenting and receiving in turn
gifts from the royal courts

3.   Late Palatial Period, 1700-1400 BC

And when the earthquakes roiled in 1700
destroying all three central palaces
you rebuilt more elaborate, spacious ones
full of storage rooms
monumental entrances
staircases, lightwells, vast courts
rooms with many doors
to keep you cool in summer
closed for heat in winter

and more amazing murals.

You covered floors and walls with
gypsum and alabaster
supported horizontal roofs,
with wooden beams
built into porous blocks
to resist future earthquakes
new columns as slender and tapering
as the ritual processional bearers
decorating Knossos' long entrance hall

Below,
where old men now cluster selling
toy flutes, fresh figs and grapes
your summer residence shimmered
for the kings of Phaestos
the villa at Agia Trianda

Your pottery now blossoms, explores
flowers and fish designs
long limbed octopi, cuttlefish, tritons
starfishes, rocks and algae,
along with delicate branching limbs,
papyrus flowers and lilies
the vases long and elegant
the urns covered with winding spiral reliefs,
round, all-knowing eyed medallions

But your snake goddess haunts,
small and great-armed statues
large stiff, explosive forms
sinuous snakes in her head
around her body, bare bosomed
like you, her worshipers.

Always the graceful bull-acrobat
the Minoan court sport,
a youth leaping over the back
of a frothing bull
your civilization's holy symbol,
liquid and active.

Then the bullhead itself:
a rhython or libation vessel
formed steatite,
inlaid eyes of rock crystal
eyelids of jasper
muzzle a pearl oyster.

On all your vessels strut the everyday processions
lively, life-loving:
court boxers stancing, a bull in gallop,
an acrobat leaping over its head and horns
agricultural tools hugging harvesters' shoulders
followed by priests and musicians,
two youth enacting a ceremonial sacrifice
or only children duplicating parental piety.

The frescoed walls of reconstructed Knosso:
the elegant Blue Bird,
among veined rocks
roses, irises, rich vegetation,
partridges in a garden beside
an altar of white lilies and red irises
from your Queen's megoran,
fanciful blue dolphins and fish
swimming among rocks
sea urchins and algae

Delicate, small miniatures
showing priestesses
dancing in an olive grove,
men and women gathering
as if awaiting an epiphany

Frances Garrett Connell

The massive bull fight
the mammoth snorting bull
the elegant Blue Ladies of Knossos
with long expressive eyes
and snaking locks,
the hundred slender youths
and priests carrying offerings,

all pieced together meticulously
the fragments 3500 years old
but faithful, as is done by twin brothers
to your day's delicate craftsmen,
rising a thousand strong
to rethink their ideas,
reset each jewel.

SAMARIA GORGE

❧

August 8, 1974

You had but to walk
from the top of a world
that created gods and legends
at Xeloshalon,
down to the sea

out into dawn
down the cliff trail
wind-teased pine trees humming
needles fragrant
into valleys of thyme, marjoram,
mountain tea
over clear running streams
and pure springs
to wind eight miles
through rock walls 1,000 feet high
past the ghost town of Samaria
to the Libyan Sea,
Aghiri Romelli's
blue-blessing waters.

But it absorbs you, barren of directions
no real path marked, just going on
never knowing if it will take you
up or down

for five hours weaving rocks and stones
back and forth over a gliding stream
or through the narrow steep walls
of the Portes

sculpted from the ancient river,
the Mediterranean's basin
bristly glaciers pulling back
fracturing earthquakes,
the dolomite rock juts out, angled,
the strata gray and tan, textured and pocked
karstic, a frayed, tight woven sheath
cloaking the earth,

into and out the whispering forest
past some abandoned cottage
or the bright, sun-drenched dry riverbeds
pocketing white rocks and pebbles
opening up to a sizzling meadow

our eyes catch, dismiss
a rustle, a distant form the color of the rock
the kri-kri Cretan goat
stays aloof,

we strain to find the rarest bearded vulture
wings broad as two men head to head
an orange underbelly like a neon sign
it drops the bones it feeds on from high up,
then spirals down to ingest the smallest pieces.

At the end we bargain with a tubby ferryman
to take us to Chora Sfaklan
to swim, to drink
then back by bus to Chania
to lap seascent and olive oil

and hear that Nixon has resigned.

SEEKING THE SORCERERS

ᏀᏋ ᏋᏁ

Just off the ferry in Iteaa
we take a VW's offer
for a ride up the hill

a professor of European history
and his wife from Ohio
steer the sharp turns
to the cluster of hotels and shops,
ancient Delfi in Parnassus' shadow.

By night
we study a golden sliver of moon
arched over the misty vault
below us.

Morning raises up,
we mount the Holy Road
past votive offerings
for victory across the known world:

temples, springs
clutching the mountainside
in the earth's cleavage
among pine groves, bleak rocks
and olive groves.

Seeking the source of the oracle
snakelike we wind
up to the demolished floor of the Temple
where the Pythia sat on a sacred tripod
imbibing herbal odors to give out secrets,

we scan fourth century grafitti,
"know thyself" "seek moderation in all things,"
drink the clear cold water
from the rocks of Kirphis

above eerie lighted red rocks,
reflect Podine and Ilemhopriko
beneath the Fedriods
two enormous gray towers
brood over the whole valley
angling the sanctuary.

Continuing up
we seek the mountain haven,
walking eleven hours
ducking sun, seeking shade
in sparsely wooded slopes
wide checkerboard fields,
the road bending
back up and over
the mountain

to the Korycean Cave
a dank earth belly where priestesses
performed Bacchic orgies.

By flashlight we see stalactites
jaws of dithonic forces
breathe in dankness,
then watch the sky:

there are no eagles circling
no one else searching
for the center of the world.

When we climb down
the sun shimmers,
a mellow rose eye.

Frances Garrett Connell

FELLOW TRAVELERS

What became of the black-robed priest
tending a watering hose behind his church in Chania,
the two girls skipping rope in the dingy alley
narrow and waste-filled between crumbling
back harbor houses?

Or the three young guards at the town museum
who never turned on the lights
(was it because it was a free day?)
as we moved in dusky halls

past Minoan vases and axes
sarcophagi, funeral reliques
as if stumbling, fingering them all
in their first dark earth niches?

And the tombstones of Turkish conqueors
relegated to the ruins behind the bushes
in the dry courtyard beside the toilets?

Or the three American girls and their mother
at Cape Sounion who sang folk songs
as we floated, stroking water like liquid silk
far below the temple crowding the cliffs?

Or Vari's villagers
roasting a hundred lambs
behind restaurant windows
for the pre-August 15th
Feast of the Assumption of the Virgin?

What of the cages of peacocks and canaries,
the pond of swans under centuries-rooted oaks,
the lemon trees swimming greenly in the air
as we waited to board

the white giant of the ferry boat
forming finally
a candelabra in the midnight black?

ON THE ORIENT EXPRESS FROM
ATHENS TO TEHRAN

ลงว ครา

August 1974

"Ha'arat" means memories.

I.

The first night passes,
we are five in the hard-seated second class compartment

The Greek student, Dionysus, looks up
from his politics, philosophy and literature
to ask in perfect English"
"Why does the American system, with all its good people
can keep turning out such bad leaders?

The CIA supported the junta dictatorship,
also Makaris collapse in Cyprus—"
He shakes his head. *"There's little difference*
in terms of using other countries
for their profit, between Russia and the U.S.,
except their flags."

Now his eyes are holding back tears.
"More than 1,000 students
were killed by tanks (most manned by the students' peers)
at the Polytechnic last November. Why?"

Later he reads us Cavafy's "Ithaka"
for its perfect thought,
"Greeks have always struggled
to maintain their land against invaders."

At Thessaloniki, a mute French fellow,
and an elderly Greek detrain.
Dionysius explains the man had been a farmer,
self-taught himself physics and electricity

authored a book on earth's origins
from glowing celestial mass.

"There is a story in each face," we confirm

Sometime near dark on the first Monday
the seating shifts
Dionysius gets off at Souflio
where he's to spend two days with his brother
stationed at the border.

Beyond Ankara
we sleep two nights
rolled up like dawnless chickens
barely distinguishing between
faces, the land, villages.

Yoni (Ionnes), born of Greek parents
in Turkey, livied there all of his life
studies now at Ankara's poly tech.

A German, two Italians, a sullen Spanish boy
pass in and out our compartments
we split bread, resume our strange postures
share a joke.

In the dining car
a retired American and his wife
who've lived in Cos for three years
bewail the sudden Greek coldness
to American yachtsmen

In a hired car, along the southeast coast of Turkey
they'd gasped at mountain cliff roads,
how lumber was laced together
and rolled to the sea.

The whole train stops.
It will be another day before it moves.

II.

On the train from Istanbul to Tehran
a wild-haired Iranian, his thin, yellow-haired
cherubic-faced German wife,
and two-year old son
hover between our compartment
and the next.

Riding through a desolate land
in an air conditioned train
is like watching a movie of another place
a long growing story
the windows firmly sealed
between ourselves and the land:

women in slacks,
rough cotton skirts and leggings.
gypsy tied bright scarves
hold babies,
men and boys uniform in slacks
rough cotton shirts
with pub-like ham caps over their

closely cropped heads
bend in a field
beside a factory
on a road strung with cars and buses
mirage-like, paralleling us
on the dry horizon

almost to the Iranian border
young groves like children
dense dry hills and tilled plains
vignettes of older ages
tiny railroad towns clustering beside the rails
murals of people laboring.

Inside our compartment other tales unwind:
The Iranian's German wife
clasping her dimpling,
quick brown-eyed child
her husband and his friends off,
as usual, comes, goes, sits shyly.

Monika, 17, met her husband
in an old German woman's flat in Hamburg
Ignorant of the *"anti-baby pills"*
the inevitable followed.
Her family disowned her,
after she took up with the Iranians.

Now she and Issie. Jr. look to Iran
to get a new family, to find work.
But she and her husband quarrel a lot.
He threw away his ring,
she lost hers in another row.
He said he's glad to have nothing
to make the world think I'm his wife.

In the next compartment,
a sleek, petted Iranian girl
a Tabriz family, Turkish-Iranians
loudly occupy the whole place
critique this German's kafir-ness
her immorality in their superior tongue.

As children do, quickly,
she catches their expressions,
communicates feelings
without words, to strangers—
eyes brimming with tears,
pale hands clutching her stomach.

While little Issie plays,
she sits with us
laughing, lauding friends,
showing snapshots, books.
Later, her husband stomps in
scolds her, ordering she return
to the next room again.

In the long night's wait while car by car
the train is loaded
onto the ferry to cross Lake Van
we hear him shouting,
Stay here with your son, shut your mouth.
Women like you can't go out.

In the morning, in our seats, she looks off,
This is not him. Then contradicts:
I was always alone, all day long
in the Hamburg room.
He didn't like me to go out
or talk with neighbors.

Issie's family was rich once
but he squandered his inheritance
on his friends, on a big American car,
unable to stomach school or naval service
then drifted to Germany's cities
to drive a cab.

More than anything I want to study, to work.
I've seen poor people's hard lives,
I'll be patient and understand the Iranians,
Issie's family.
I always worked, to support my mother.
She slept with too many men.

All the next day
her husband taunts her:
Ask this woman to exchange beds with me.
I shouldn't have to sleep
with women and children next door.

He prowls the corridor past midnight
waiting for me to settle down
in either my lawful berth
or the one he would delegate.
I stay in my own place
barely asleep when the whole crew

minus the mother and son
thump against the door
giggling in demented Persian
about having to sleep in this manner.
At five the father is still stalking the aisles
a stormy spoiled toddler turned pouter.

Day three, at noon,
we are all tumbled out
into the Tehran station's crowds,
sharp-featured faces, dark eyes stare
from thin cotton shawls binding figure, head
families and wrapped bundles spread out.

Over her shoulder, Monika waves,
grins, holds her son's wobbly arm:

swept on, we nod,
consider prayer.

BUS ACROSS IRAN, AUGUST 1973

ଊଉ ୯ଌ

In the mobbing Tehran train station
crowds study the Asia Games on TV
It is another holy day.
From nowhere young Hossain and his sister-cousin
offer to find us a hotel,
pull us to their East German car
to madly scramble through "modern" Tehran
He's a last year student of Economics
she works with Iranian-American oil
their brothers, cousins live in Florida and California

We take a simple hotel,
all the others booked
along with all flights, trains, buses
for a week to Meshed
except one third-rate company's fleet,
set to leave at 10:00 a.m. the next day.

Restless all night, we board in a dirty alley
fidget as the bus leaves the city, is sent back;
the driver has no license, or forgot his bribe.
We sit inside the Palace of Justice's courtyard
until another bus arrives,
just as this first driver bursts out,
clutching his papers.

A man working in Kuwait
shares his common language and chocolate bars
as we move over desert and valley, into night
people litter the floors, boys vomit
children stretch like corpses across the aisles
to sleep

At a stop for dinner and prayer
we watch our driver, doped on pills and hashish
chanting woozily.
He'll stay awake for 26 hours
until we sputter into Meshed
prayers loud and clear,

de-bus,
and head right out

JAPAN, *2010*

BARE ABOVE BERING STRAIT

Singular, it can not be.

Naked and arched,
like this plane's trajectory
over the bald pate of the round globe
we're somewhere south of the Arctic Circle
above Russio-Asia, Kamchutka's rills,
the jutting Shirshov Ridge,
five and a half hours yet to Tokyo.

A lip of the rising sun kisses
our dip over the North Pole
land masses rooted
in Echo Bay,
ferocious glacial fields
startled distant white peaks
among tumescent cloud banks.

Our plane tracking—
no longer than a screen view
the sky map angles,
swoops down to Cape Dezhnev,
Cape Prince of Wales,
we hover between Nome
and Chukotka,

flared wings shadow,
the Chukchi and Bering Seas,
a pebble dropped in a well
the International Date Line
severs Big and Litte Diomede
islands in the middle where
21 hours separate a kilometer.

A bird on a string
we glide,
ready to be jerked again
to a circular projection.

A Japanese House

I would be a traditional Japanese house
flexible as wood and paper
adaptable in my interior spaces

I would keep a warm *irori* hearth
in the dwelling's heart
protected in a sunken floor
surrounded by rice-woven *tatami*
as elegantly simple as those gracing
sparse temple gates
I'd give room to the earth, the transitions,
in my dirt-pocked dome,
where all the world could pause,
move toes to circulate, shoeless

before they stepped inside
freshly come from the *engawa*
the verandah where air flows and pounds
under a protective sloping roof
revealed like magic when my wooden doors—
sustenance and soul—
moved gracefully open.

I'd finely craft the formal *tokonomi*,
the well-floored alcove where my flowers,
the scroll of my life,
sheltered its content
I varied each season

Frances Garrett Connell

Light would flood my rooms
through the paper-thin *fusuma,*
visitors would kneel on rush and straw
tatami six deep,
rustling still with imagined breezes
in unharvested fields
in late summer.

Warmth would permeate from a *kotatsu*
where thoughts, dreams,
memories, and my family
would gather around the table
of my love.

Overhead
marking the smallest separations
would be the perfect crafting of beams,
wooden lintels,
layers of ceilings and shelves
like hidden dreams

every part to bend and fold
to give itself to change.

ASAKUSA

෨ ෫

It's at the end of the train line
twenty minutes from the house where I stay
but I'd been walking there since dawn,

trying to imagine two fishermen's pleasure,
pulling up Kannon from tangled Sumida River nets,
1400 years ago,
picturing miracles in the splattered drops
before the holy man Shokai
sheltered this compassionate goddess
in the temple, Senso-ji,

wondering what mercy she granted them,
these fishers of goddesses
when an imperial census, the *taika*
made them serfs, declared all land, labor, soldiering
for the emperor,
when the Paekche's king's blossoming Buddhism
coupled with nature-magic Shintoism

to insure peace for present and future lives,
how Prince Shoroku and the Empress
imported Chinese ways—city plans,
fine silk, lacquer, porcelain,
asking what pleasure came to this quarter
rife with many a millennium later,
when famine piled up 90,000 dead

shrinking Edo further
with cholera's swift waters,
so the government called for
fireworks along the Sumida
to provide repose
for the souls of the dead,
to drive away the scourge.

Now amusement parks,
pinball and video games, *panchinko* galleries,
clutter the curving lanes beyond the river,
as I move under Nakamise-dori's covered alleys,
past densely-covered trinket shops,
stalls sweet with rainbow-perfect rice confections,
goddesses, towers, sculpted in perfect miniature,

amid the practical,
the imitated,
from vendor's slippers
to raincoats
to Godzilla dolls,
for visitors
and pilgrims.

Closer to the shrine, the traditional lingers,
things too beautiful to touch:
washi, exquisite hand-made paper
for epistles and origami,
reproductions of *ukiyo-e*, woodblocks of the floating world,
geisha silks and regal kimonos,
lacquer ware,

brushes, ink and ink stones, obi sashes, dolls,
fans, *chiyogami,* wrapping papers rich as pearls,
masks and amulets, figurines
afloat in religious statues, dolls,
paper and bamboo pieces,
elegantly boxed
kaminori okoshi crackers.

At Kaminarimon Gate,
I duck under the shouldering *toriis,*
the thunder god guardians,
Fujin and Roijin, emboldened,
pass the *chochin,* story-high lanterns,
as pilgrims imbibe healing fumes
at the massive incense dispensers,

they dole out 100 yen
at the *omikuji* stalls
to open the oracle,
see querants shake sticks
then read out the answers matched
from 100 possible drawers
in metal containers.

In another courtyard
the Nadi-Botokesena Buddha perches delicately,
head and stomach glow, polished by worshippers
seeking health and luck,
while the ancient Bensen-yama *shoro,*
settles under wooden house and stone cover
miming the hours it used to ring eons ago.

I weave over elfin stone bridges
between gardens and narrow streams
thick with golden carp *(koi)*
following the covered water route
running through gravel, sand,
and water lilies,
to the scattered reconstructed temples,

pull up scarf,
tuck hands in pockets,
before statues of Buddhas,
great teachers, guardians and liberators
covered with coats, gloves and hats
like forgetful children,
this winter day.

Another garden, walled,
dances with Basho's haiku
a statue commemorates Chuki Keroba
who served the poor and educated girls,
others remember great artists like
Izumo no Okunia,
father of Kabuki.

In the dragon-backed main pavilion,
fierce-faced deities stare through gold lotuses and angels,
each sanctified space, between statue, stepping stones,
flowers, cleansing dipper, a bow,
tossing of coins, a supplication,
another bow,
a head full of incense.

Circling back out
the two storied Hazo-mon Gate,
under huge lanterns, I stretch,
reach up to the over-sized sandals.

Legend claims their straw,
once touched,
insures I'll walk
propitiously, forever.

VISITING THE LAND OF TANI BUNCHO
(1763-1840)

෨ ෬

I am inside his landscape dizzily
enacting strokes of the Izu Peninsula—

canopying pine trees, up-cropped stone islands,
meandering path to a mountain retreat

curve of blue bay and brown sand,
fishing hut, mirror water,

storm-approaching sky—
rendered alive, touchable, resonate.

Son of a poet, a *samurai* by inheritance
his Bunjinga literati style

embraced Chinese, Japanese,
and Western art.

Daoist Immortals dance and melt,
as motion full as candlewax.

Outside, the sea laps land
timeless and tender.

KamaKura

୧୬ ⸙୭

a.   The Great Buddha

In this seaside town of limping temple-shrines
wood-frame houses settle under steep tile roofs.
Old courtesans and young priests lisp,
call delicately from patterned gardens and lattice fences,
beckon pilgrims to mount the staircases,
enter ancient cypress *torii* gateways
that carve out the clouds and shade
of Jufu-ji, Jochi-ji, and Hachiman-ji.

Behind the Daibutsu,
still brassy and tranquil after 758 years
his full four-dozen feet
withstand seismic shakes
atop four copper lotus leaf shock absorbers.

I weave among a middle school group
garbed like Commodore Perry's naval officers
or the Imperial Russian army.
As their Ipods zing,
they buy bracelet charms, modern netsuke.

In the garden
elderly volunteers tend the temple.
Straw-shoe footed, in pilgrim wrap,
a slight man catches my eye, then whispers
secrets in perfect war-veteran English,
"Korean lanterns have three levels,
the Japanese mini-pagoda ones, six."

Smiling, he points to a stone,
"The tanka inscribed on the rock,
praises the Great Buddha's 500th year."
He leads me further,
watching where my feet land,
to show the quarter-ton base stones
now holding statues.
"They came to rest here after a typhoon
destroyed everything else."

b.   Wandering between Temples

Back alleys lead to the edge of hills
holding wooden houses, braided timber
arched porches and screens,
up past the Hosedera Temple's 11-faced Kannon.
Along the Great Buddha Hiking Trail,
shrines overrun by red foxes
ask benedictions for children,
the buried, the needy.

Up the mountain at Zusen-ji Tangi
new camellias and flowering plum adorn,
at Zen Arai Bento Shrine
the goddess of musical eloquence and the arts reigns.
Below shrines and coves
the springs tunnel further under passageways,
bubble up where people wash their coins:
legend promises wealth to cleaned money.

Up to the garden atop the town,
across grounds, down steep stepping stones
over empty woods, to more streams and gullies,
fir-lined craft shops make wooden block prints,
porcelain and pottery, weave elegant cloth,
carve pine medallions,
birth mythological creatures.

From Kita-Kamkura's simple Zen temples
and its master Engaki-ji,
I look down to Tokei-ji
once a nunnery,
a retreat for wives fleeing their husbands.
If its asylees lived austerely there
for three reclusive years,
they earned freedom, a divorce.

Below me spreads the Ken Cho-yi:
its garden forms the character for mind and heart.
Under giant sprawling trees—juniper and pine—
the locals hold *hasen kuyo,*
memorial for *chasen,* utensils from the tea ceremony.
In one cave the Happy Buddha
guards over tiered graves.

Before the 730 years old Byakusin tree
I bow instinctively,
then stroll back to Kamakura
where it all began.

KYOTO, 2010

᠙ᢍ ᡗᢓ

i.　　Approach
Last night's snow powder-sugared Tokyo.
Inside the gliding Shinkasen, the windows shine,
beyond Shin Yokahama
rugged white dusted ranges
escort noble Fujiyama like guards.
In dawn's first light,
they ashen pine green slopes.

Past Shizroka's fragile pose,
city perched to host the next earthquake,
perfectly manicured,
verdant tea and rice terraces
lead up to unexplored, untamed trees
round village houses, farmlands
in the Southern Alps.

Below, the plain spills out the modern sprawl,
Hamanatsu, Nagayo,
Kyoto.

ii.　　Temples
East and west, past
Harachukumachji, and Shoki Street
the Eastern and Western area
temples shimmer in silence,

mountains cup on three sides
as the Kamo River bisects
encroaching woods,
torii gates command each element,
recall the founder's Heian-kyo,
Capital of Peace and Tranquility,

draw one to nod under gates,
touch basin, call out to flowing water,
in well-shaped gardens
wanderer and pilgrim shed shoes,
whisper, bow before carved eaves
scatter pathways between statues, stone lanterns

scented with dark seasoned cedar
smoking incense rings,
before unseeing golden gods, amulets and fortunes,
pulled into form and meaning
in dark chambers' histories
under curved canopies of open sky.

To stench pestilence and cure disease—
the thinking went
as artisans and farmers settled by the river,
scooped out homes as miniature as *tatami* mats,

braided wood, potted fires under floors
made every surface mutable for storage or sitting,
appeased gods who'd luxuriated in trees, brook, well, rock
long before the people broached them—
city dwellers must make festivals, rituals, temples,
to honor spirits capable of fury or rare kindness.

Frances Garrett Connell

For a thousand years fires burned,
earth shook, wars leveled,
governments came and left,
the city rebuilt.

In the Gian
women with wax skins, silk robes,
glanced out from under pompadoured locks
sculpted in delicate buns
wove between temples and teahouses,
wooden inns and shops

strolled clip-clop on high wooden shoes,
on flagstone and cobblestone-
laid Ishibe-Kobe Lane
and its sisters,

to secret gardens and chambers
courting civility,
connecting years and dynasties with
haikus of delicate moth wings,
stringed instruments
that whispered heartbeats.

From the Palm of the Hand Museum
the Ne-he-No Michi Avenue passes galleries,
clothes shops and jewelers,
down long stone staircases beneath Kodai-ji.

Past the Ryoben Kabban, Maruyama Park,
up and down Sannenzaka and Ninezaka
to vermilion and concrete *torii* gates
where, this 4th of February, hanging on winter's last thread,
priests and priestesses in brocade robes and liturgy,
bow to ancient paced musician's bells,

flutes, drums and dancers,
then rain down beans on hungry crowds
as bingo-lottery vendors exchange chances
for household prizes.

iii. Kiyomizu-dera
Mount the temple grounds.
One thousand years of pilgrims
climbed these steep hills
to pray before 11-headed Kannon of Mercy,
drink bubbling spring water to restore health
to bow and gasp politely before the main hall:
before majestic aerial porch, veranda crafted without a nail
like wood woven into one cloak.

Pass sweet shops,
booths making porcelain as multi-colored
as peacock tails, painted fans
narrating seasons and Genji liaisons,

the temple precarious over plunging ravine
its cantilevered roofs majestic:
peripheral shops sell love charms,
statues to rub, emblematic deities,
directions for sealing preferred relationships
here where the stand from which
older generation, dishonored,
"jumped off Kiyuomizu's stage."

On the winding path down.
staring out of green eyes,
a brown-capped monk beseeches,
prays before an open bowl.

iv. Kodaiji
Perfectly balanced, a widow's condolence
braid roof and ceiling
tight as wheat checks

house Hiyoshi and Nene's silky rippling dragons
prowling in pine and bamboo knolls.
coal-eyed, shaggy-coated tigers.

The ancient temple hall's,
shadowy enamel and black
gold and red lacquer
spiral arching wood

teahouses scattered like chess pieces
among moss and vine-covered staircases,
arching bridges, graceful bamboo forests,
nested chrysanthemums abloom.

Man, fate, nature,
etched, in a dry garden at Daisen
gravel and rock waterfalls recall earth,
heaven, the mountain Horat where life began,
a wall, the barrier, human hesitations,
the barrier to any embracing life
then a river, life itself, sand and rocks,
as a turtle swims upstream.

At Kodaiji, the vast ocean's waves
impeccably raked gravel
settle calm, frozen, meditative,
pull the eyes to two cone-shaped mounds
a small balboa tree in the corner.

v. Zen temples and tea ceremonies
Ryonaji is rusticity,
understatement
clay walks,
raked sand,
fifteen rocks

Ginkaku-ji's
Hall of Emptied Mind atop
the silent Tower of Sand Waves,
is entered only through
the long tall rows of edging hedges

The Sound of Feather Waterfall
tumbles high up behind the terraced garden's shrines
to Jizo, 100 stone images
protecting dead children and travelers.

vi. Kinkajuji, Golden Temple
Once a villa in the northern hills,
cusped windows and ornamental roof
a Chinese phoenix struts above its eaves,
it dazzles, this gold covered pavilion,
toy-staged shrines, bush-cloven wooden teahouses,
beside the lake, among gardens and wandering steps
leading to running water.

MEIJI SHRINE, JANUARY 2010

It is about sanctuaries, totems
kami housed in *ronde:*
nature spirits in foxy-eared statues,
the emperor's own lineage to the Sun.

Sunday, off the Chiyoda Line,
I join the salutations to the man, sun-god, emperor
who westernized the country
wrote *waka,* toasted huge barrels
of Bourgogne wine and saki.

I bound five steps across a bridge
skirting the Yoyogi Park amid pine forests,
parade under shadowed 1700-year old cypress,
through the torii's (gates) to the hut
where pilgrims catch the dipper,
bob it in the sacred pool,
wash one, then the other hand.

In the outer courtyard,
supplicants write out poems on wooden plaques
hang them one by one on hooks on the sheltered stall,
to be set before the shrine that day,
to seek a divination.

Beyond the massive trees
surrounding the courtyard corners and shrine
I climb stairs to the inner courtyard
pierced by its winglike green-copper roof,
gabled cypress wood pillars.

Out from the wrapping portals and arches,
winds a wedding procession,
the priest in silver crowned hat
billowing pants, apron, tunic,
the bride in white kimono
inches on shoes like small platforms.
In the center, guests in dark suits wait.

Along the path, the Jings Waien,
the Emperor's garden, is bare this season,
his favorite iris blossoms,
silent, spilling down a slop
from the weathered teahouse,
to where simple wooden benches
edge a fishing pond
home to golden carp the size of kittens.

Another path leads to the mysterious well
dressed in sheets of woven branches
and steep-pitched roof.

At Kaguradon Hall, *samesen* and *koto*
twang melodies, before military bands.
The Otori, the Treasure House,
shows portraits of every Emperor
for a thousand years,
beside Victorian stable's,
a modern Gymnasium
shaped like a Samurai's helmet.

In the Harajuku District across the street
youth roam.
Costume-toting, they move
in rivers of shouldering relevance.
Today's fad is Little Bo Peep outfits,
girls like painted Dresden dolls,
boys with purple spikes of hair.
They line up at shops touting crepes stuffed
with a hundred kinds of ice cream,
Japanese-redefined bagels
flavored with white chocolate chips
and green tea.

Comanche-style, the scream of traffic pierces:
we are all secular pilgrims,
in redefined western clothes.

A red sun settles low
beyond a sparse fringe of trees
and secured gates.

Frances Garrett Connell

MIMIZUKU MOUND

᎙᎙ Ꮛ᎙

(from 1592-1598)

Somewhere in the neighborhoods
behind the Tokyo Station
the high mound rises
left from its enshrinement
in the reign of "the unifier," Hideyoshi.

Thirty-eight thousand
Korean noses and ears
harvested by generals
shipped in barrels of brine
following a victory in Chosun.

These the prizes left, exchanged
for the army's payment,
the others' parts counted and discarded,
too many dead this time to ship whole,
as severed heads,

just the noses, just the ears,
received, recorded, rewarded,
the unnamed skin
in its humanly-defined shape,
given a Buddhist burial in this tomb.

A SHOMODA HISTORICAL WALKING TOUR

Down the Izu peninsula,
to Odawara, Atami and Ito,
tiny packed hamlets

their orange and blue roof tiles
notes nestled between cliffs
languishing at mountain's bowl bottom
like too-sweet broth left over from a stew
falling to gravel-edged ocean,
flicked with outcrop islands of stone.

To Shomoda's fishing village:
pastel wooden warehouses, latticed shops
white-grid houses of black slate,
rise along remnant cobblestone lanes
as muffin-tin round hills,
cut between the standing history.

This gray-clouded Sunday afternoon
I pace the places, for tragic stories,
recall Perry's seven "Black Ships,"
opening up Japan in 1854,
the temple honoring young Okichi,
at 15 made to serve "the foreigner,"

ostracized,
she drowned herself in the Inozawa River
glistening past the Shinto Shrine
where *taika-bashi* drummers pound and circle
through red and golden arches,
sweaty faces shining under benign-faced Buddha.

Next door a blooming plum tree,
acres of American jasmine trees,
mark Gyokuseng's first consulate,
the first cow slaughtered to eat,
the first cow milk drunk,
Perry's signature for 'Peace and Harmony.'

The old black market,
once raucous with bottleshops, prostitutes,
contraband for sailors
is turned now to teahouses
serving local netted fish
along a willow-draped river.

Hardy early camellias flood the park above the town.
From among the pine woods,
blooming hydrangea, strewn statues,
terrace a miniature harbor,
open to show seven shrouded islands
down Ura Promenade.

At the Aquarium
sea turtles swim silently
in a circular pool,
paddle boats and kayaks sweep
between dolphins
in corralled off blue waters.

A *gassimo*-style folk farm house
raises steep thatch roof like praying hands
pulls up folk scenes of snowy mountains
tiny humans trudging paths
as sheer and breakable as ice planks
over peak after peak.

From the evening train back to Yokohama
I see hills full of orange trees
fruit luminescent as a million rising suns.

UENO PARK, TOKYO

ॐ ☙

(January 2010)

Mondays the museums close,
so I scout out the free shrines,
profuse as an Irish bard's tale
in the well-texted manuscript
of this formal park,

skirt edges of the Kaoi-ji temple,
Tokugawa's medicine against evil spirits,
plow between the Toshi-gu's 100 stone lanterns,
under renovation, so only a painted front,
the Chinese gates, stands real,

bow at the eternal flame to banish nuclear war,
beside the five-story pagoda
enshrined among peacocks and elephants
in the Children's Zoo.

Too old to leave prayers
in the conception-blessing Kiyo-mizu Hall
populated by shiny-checked dolls,

I grin at the foxes guarding
down-winding archways,
where tiny woven straw huts
hood bursts of peonies.

Beneath a grove of willows
sumptuous flutes and wooden keys rise,
a Peruvian group, Mazamuara,
carries us to the Andes.

Around the corner,
a bagpiping-diabolist entices
with "Amazing Grace,"
a crowd giggles and gawks,
as he spins tops in the air.

Around the Shinebazu pond,
wizened, silent elders nap in the sun
while others photograph
darting yellow-wings,
purple martins singing in the trees.

Plump felines snuggle on benches,
hunker under hedges.
A crow, large as a baby lion,
caws,
mysterious.

HATAJUKU

ಲ ಲ

English characters dance on the sign,
as the bus burrows down the mountain from Hakone
dropping locals off at narrow villages,
like carved chess pieces
to perch on the collapsed earthquake
vents in steamy outcroppings, hot springs.

I read of the exquisite *yogegi-zaiku* woodwork
mosaic boxes made for a thousand years:
the strips cut from different trees,
glued into large blocks
then shaped on lathes to bowls and boxes,
lacquered, filled with magic secrets.

Intrepidly, I bathe at the *onisen*,
test scalding water, balance towel on head,
shed inhibitions among misty women,
along with dry skin.

VIETNAM

TWENTY-THREE THOUSAND DONG
TO THE DOLLAR

Wearily, as midnight stalked,
I waved away the cabbie's words
exiting the Ho Chi Minh City Airport,
"Pay 23,000 d? Pay, yes?"
"It's prepaid already, no more" I shot back.
So he dipped in his own pocket and flashed the dong
to pass out the gate.

His English a few nouns, my Vietnamese nonexistent,
we drove silently through streets
where motorbikes whizzed and lurched
in inky darkness splotched by neon illuminations
hobbled together shops, animated marquees,
signs advertising airlines, liquor, and government bureaus,
old men bent over card games on stoops
lighted by their chain-smoking like fireflies.

Shaking his head,
marking me as yet another imperialistic ugly American,
he dumped me and my overfed knapsack
on a fecund avenue 20 minutes later,
pointed to a dark covered alley
wedged between tiny hotels, their signs out:
"Pham-Ngu-Lai," he shouted, and drove away

I stroked a reservation in my pocket, the address.
War waged here by my land dragged away my youth,
led a brother to insanity, made me want only peace.

But, a Judas, not even for silver, or a Messiah
I'd squandered all honor for folded bills,
23,000 dong:
less than one U.S. Dollar.

SCENES AROUND HANOI

෴

1.   Lenin Park and the Flag Tower

Remnant of the old city's guard station
razed by the French in punishment,
it stands, Hanoi's symbol.

Across the whirling boulevard
a park spreads, a fountain shadows
well-kept red and golden zinnia flowerbeds,
a life-size Lenin scowls:
the roller-blading boys lunching there
barely glance at the legacy.

2.   Lovers on the Bridges Leaving Hanoi

We move
on invisible threads
to board assigned compartments
on the Reunification Express
as the night whips over us

when the train crosses the Red River:
in the narrow niches
on the pedestrian lane
lovers bend secretly
into each other.

3. One Pedestal Pagoda

Dwarfish, it is sacred
connoting an emperor who found an heir
by marrying a servant girl:
another father of a nation
through the common folk.
Shaped like a lotus flower,
the original shattered in revenge
when the French left,
this duplicate opens up to us.

4. Old Quarter

In the Old Quarter
street vendors wedge each other
their lane's special merchandise
inherited from medieval guilds
but the items changed,
route made, electrified,
Hang plus product for each domain:

jewelry, silk, tinware, pots and pans,
cosmetics, cloth, spices, timber,
furniture, funeral banners, engravings,
grain, ceremonial shrines, fake money
(for burning as part of ancestor worship)
medicine, massages, temple gifts, shoes, mats
food.

Now added tourist guides, electric gimmickry,
toys of every origin and standard, trinkets,
cookies and baked goods, phone stores,
mannequins touting fake designer belts
purses, bags, dresses, and shoes,
jeans, shirts,
a handful of sleek cut silks,

a pile of embroidered antiques.

ON THE TIP OF CHINA BEACH

ॐ ॐ

At Cua Dai I pose on driftwood
edging the South China Sea,
nibble sandy wind, pounding surf
five kilometers outside Hoi An.

Tortoise shell round fishing boats
their nets and floats secret armor
tucked under damp wood,
stretch off to the horizon.
Straight east, the Cham Islands form,
their round mound silhouettes
distinct in the misty
cloud-laden waters.

Windblown to oblivion,
craving this sea warm as a bathtub
I huddle at the end of the 30 kilometer sweep
G.I's called "China Beach,"
lined now by small, thistle thatch huts,
resorts under construction.

But if you turn your back to them
just walk south or north,
tread wave, surf, litter, combed sand
you face a sea
eternal and unformed
innocent as time's beginning.

CA CHI TUNNELS, MARCH 13, 2010

Fitting, a sobering end
to a 60's American protester's journey.

Fed first a simple rice porridge,
a newsreel propaganda film,
we watch humans navigate
three to four-level underground tunnels
by scooting earthworm flat
on their bellies

schoolgirls in crisp school blouses man M-54s
dangle long braided plaits with ribbons
as they plant explosives like Easter eggs
along jungle trails to trap
the evil Americans, like bad tigers,
the video tells,

they forced a peaceful people to hide in the earth
to labor by night
to sustain their land and country.

(Scour alive the leaders,
who dispatch the young to die
infuse them with false hope and passion
but spare the people, one flesh.)

The Vietcong-clad guide
not even born when the War ended,
grins and leads us to the bomb craters,
arms assembly workshops, drop trap doors,
pits with spikes to impale intruders who mis-step
(how sick our human ways of killing,
maiming each other),

past manikins of Vietminh and Vietcong,
guarding, recycling scavenged U.S. Armaments,
in co-ed rest areas, like fashion manikins,
kitchen, briefing and strategy rooms.
He demonstrates hidden entrances
camouflaged like ant hills

At a scripted 100-meter stretch
we enter the dark, hot earth,
on hands and knees paw in the dark
from Level 1 to Level 2,
inching through the memory

of the tiny, driven people
who sustained this defense system,
lived there for years at a time
against French, then American fighters

the 6,000 out of 16,000 who survived
after the US forces
thinking to abate the flow of fighters and supplies
thrown back against them
bombed huge parts to smithereens.

To naught:
Vietnam a thriving capitalist country now
everything for sale
every individual an entrepreneur
the US dollar preferred over "the dong."

The wise among the residents,
like Ha, our guide, a Vietcong's son,
shrugs kindly:
"The past is the past.
We are all the same.
We must live and go on."

IN CLOUDY MOUNTAINS, ABOVE DANANG

ᏯᎧ ᏗᏬ

March 2010

Perhaps the mountain deities
still guard them at Hai Van,
brought back the vibrant green
after defoliating war

a marble sign, three Chinese words,
mark the Champa's old frontier,
"the most grandiose landscape on earth."

Beyond Cloudy Mountain to Truong Son
fog billows, shrouds.
Moss covers French-made blockhouses
where guerrilas, Vietcong, GI's

fought over DaNang,
the bunkers and the Empress fort
hulking here now like a bitter taste.

Beneath, the sea spreads,
clean sands roll out to San Truc,
and the Five Mountains.

At Danang, where bawdy sex hotels and bars
leered soldiers for a decade,
bred Amerasian children, syphilis, addicts,

private posh hotels, international chains,
golf courses, time-shares, swimming pools
hoard and claim the China Sea
south of My Khe.

Perhaps local deities
ensconced in the pass's mighty tiger,
favored the local folks,

resented the U.S. Air Force base
that sits, a skeleton behind brick and mortar walls,
where crisp-suited troops first landed in 1965,

After Saigon, Hue fell,
U.S. helicopters sent to liberate loyal governors,
over-weight with escapes,
crashed out at sea.

Below Nui Son Tra
like a pair of monkey ears,
jutting into the sea,
another failed invasion:

Spanish-led Filipino and French troops
attacked Danang in August 1858
when Tu Duc' mistreated Catholic missionaries.

The city fell, a pyrrhic victory,
past retribution, came like a scepter—
cholera, dysentery, typhus, scurvy,

mysterious fevers slayed the invaders:
one year later more dead
than 20 times those killed in combat.

We rise and fall
up roads in clouds,
strangling the green mountains.

OPERATION ROLLING THUNDER

Terse, corded as the old shopkeeper's neck
the fog loops around us on the mountain
we are on hallowed ground

an airy wetness cloaks me
as I cross the road and mount the trail
pulling along on invisible strings
the old shopkeeper, her foot dragging.

Back in her village
sprung up again these 42 years after flattening
the women's silver bracelets,
highneck plates, shine even on babies.

Flooded plots bear rice and corn
the gongs, breeze sounded,
dance across the valley
for the yearly celebration of the dead.

She stands a moment
straight as the wooden effigies
they mount on family graves

this year
will they have enough to sacrifice
a buffalo?

Pitched straw roofs, houses built on stilts
blossom like finely landed cranes
in the river valleys
among flooded rice paddies
for these Mountaineers, the Montegnards.

I've lost her face in the fog, but feel her colors
the long striped skirt, the thick hair
packed inside the tall scarf turban.

Dodging her post cards and bracelets
their bone-white painted beads suggesting gravestones,
I nod and try to climb alone toward the old French fort,
once an Imperial guard house.
then a Vietnam People's Army perch,

but she slips the stringed beads,
blue designs like Dresden china,
over my wrist.

"You, me, same?"
She has no teeth,
her English terse like bird peckings
she points to my hair, gray roots
under the thin brown rinsed curls.

"American, American? We both were little then?
The time of the endless thunder?
The time of Khe Sanh?"

Up here the clouds never left.

She's speaking now,
clearly as a cantor,
spilling out her story
among old bunkers,
faded signs for still-buried ordinance.

She'd been a child in the village,
helped on the hill coffee plantations,
off Route 9 near the Laotian border.

Her village manned by three kings,
one each for Fire, Wind, and Water,
they had lived in peace.
But daily she watched new foreigners come.
"Did you know those Americans?"

There'd been airstrips, the Special Forces
the Marines and the Green Berets,
then the thunder:

I'd read of it, but not when it happened,
not as the spillover of a secret war.
Only for its headlines:

Westmoreland's deadly tantrum
to save an unneeded Marine base
in the middle of nowhere

after the Vietnamese People's Army stood
used ground, artilleries, mortar and rocket attacks
on the combat base, and hilltops around

for 77 days
he declaimed for,
unleashed
on lush hamlets and jungles
more aerial firepower than had been seen
in all the wars before that,

each mission named like naughty boys
mocking history—
Operation Niagara, Operation Pegasus
Operation Neutralize:

40,000 tons of bombs.
4,000 airstrikes,
5,000 dead both sides, 6,000 wounded.

Old veterans like the walking dead still
hobble somewhere in America, likely homeless,
lame men lapse in doorways
in Ho Chi Minh City, Hanoi.

As monsoons raged
in every tiny village,
the hill people
massacred

if they did not escape
when the new regime came in,
missions, sorties, droppings.

'Then, kaput," she spits, looks up at me
she of the little people,
"No flying birds would take the Dro

my father, my uncle,
who'd fought for the Americans.
They all went away."

The next big man had closed the base.

The green returned, life grew
re-clothed, resurrected the bloodied,
moonscape cratered Khe Sanh.

But up here,
the clouds never left.

When I pull out bills,
pay her for the useless bracelet,
and another,
the money is wet,
as sticky as blood.

"The Bloodiest and Longest Battle of the War"

❧ ❧

1.   Hue National Cemetery and Park

Row after row
the gravestones stretch
unnamed

on emerald hills above the Perfume River,
stark pillars melt into fecund fields
past silence and horizon.

Is it like your Arlington? The guide suggests.
We wanted to give an earthly place
for those souls who have no one left.

On nights when the moon grows round
plump as an ivory plum
the spirits of those killed
leave their graves and wander.

You Americans mourn what you lost
but we lost more, three million,
a whole generation massacred.
Still, we let what was, be.

We have gone on.
He turns to me, his black eyes
descending, carrying me back to his story—
his six years training to be a monk

his father crippled as a Vietcong
unable to work, himself exiled, a boy servant
paid with meals,
a place by the door to sleep.

The spirits?
Do you see the holes atop each stone?
They leave and enter there.

2.   The Citadel

Stone by stone
they fought for these algae-stained walls,
up and down the Belvedere of the Phoenixes
to shred a red and blue flag with a yellow star
to fly high their own, their client's instead.

In this layered pavilion for a last emperor's show
where his majesty abdicated to Ho Chi Minh
sixty long years before,
they flaunted the temple drums:
the dragon-carved eaves over-hung
dripped corpses as the battle raced.
Groomed lotus ponds where carp
flash now like bits of gold
gurgled with blood.

Across the bridge
the Thai Han Palace's yellow lacquered columns
shoulder a maze of halls and courtyard walls
that hummed and paused an entry
to the Forbidden Purple City

each building flattened, stones strewn,
the emperor's jewels, the massive chambers,
gone now, only piles of coded stone
fallen inlaid ceiling vaults, pulverized walls
that mark each new interior.

Workmen hammer and restore
one room at a time,
where American A4 Skyhawks
dropped bombs and napalm
to flush out the enemy in his own land.

3.   Along the Perfume River

Beside the Perfume River
women in long stripped skirts and sandals
pole their sampans along the shore
to stalls at Dong Bai, a feverish hive.

In piercing sun, the houseboats bob,
their rooftop shrines glow softly
like tinsel on a stretched out Christmas tree.

Behind them new hotels flash steel and glass,
host imperial cuisines
served on Hue's fine porcelain,
earth-stamped and cleared of ideograms
for the columns of international tourists.

On the banks young lovers stroll
through tulip and bougainvilleas,
families picnic, squat like animated
chess pieces on the clean board
of the edged sidewalk squares,
stare and chatter
amid stone and aluminum sculptures
bending to gardens
that memorialize peace.

On Trang Tien Bridge,
pedestrians, cyclists, and cars
pass each reconstructed trestle
to move in time-lapse frames,
the flow unstinting.

Beneath, entrepreneurs change money,
book tourist boats, instantly burn photos to CDs,
on either side the skeletons of once proud Mandarin quarters
spread out a block as reclaimed terrace restaurants,

rest houses
guaranteeing cheap fresh fish, papayas,
any food piled cornucopia high
served in shimmering candlelight.

When the willowy high school girls pass
in their pure white uniforms,
dense, glossy hair waving as they stroll,
I start, thinking angels manifested
as silent children.

4.   Survivors

Are these the children, or the children of the children
the survivors of the Battle 42 years back
these hump-backed tiny women in black pajamas
frail as weeds, these chain-smoking men
shuffling feet, cards, dishes of soup

were they alive when the GI's
these foreign fighters woke up to find
they had missed a beat
came up off-guard, unprepared
in this mellow old Imperial capital
they'd encamped in
and thought invulnerable?

When the northern army swept in with dawn
reclaimed the ghostly fortress
the Americans pounced to keep the location:
they couldn't afford to lose their supply line
up Highway One from Danang
down the coastal road from the Hai Van Pass

when the Tet offensive burst all over the South
striking over 100 cities and Saigon
on that first day of the Year of the Monkey.

But Hue was to be different
a house by house urban war
street fighting for 22 days,
as both sides
riled up to make it bend
a collective head,
let thunder roar:

three thousand civilians
culled for mislaid loyalty
massacred for allegedly propping up
a puppet Southern regime

five thousand, eight thousand,
Vietcong, North Vietnam troops dead
more than 2,000 GI's killed or wounded.

Seventy percent of the city leveled,
the bowels and guts and jewels
of the once-forbidden city
flattened to rubble.

Of the more than ten bridges
spanning the Huong River and its canals
only Trang Tien claims itself
a signature:

time moved on,
under,
on its sturdy,
airy shoulders.

VIETNAMESE WATER PUPPETS

We enter the gold and black lacquered theater
wedged between bedraggled veranda-style wood shops
and the show begins:

Fanciful
in front, in tight slit skirts
drummer, flutist, string banjo lyre, female singers
sit beside a lake, the stage.

Behind
a dragon-bedazzled tile-roofed pagoda
hovers scarlet,
underneath, the curtains,
from which the puppets exit and enter.

Opening:
A ruff-headed commoner, the jokester
rushes, dances, trounces,
splashes, saunters, glides through the water
announcing with whimsy and animation

a story hard to follow
as the musicians spin sounds, lyrics
velvet, then choppy.
The youth addresses us, is addressed.

Out pour a dozen golden dragons who cavort and circle,
a fishermen and a fisherwomen flirt and struggle,
advancing, withdrawing, their nets.

A pair of peacocks give birth to a white egg,
then a new peacock,
golden carp and trout swish-swash about,
a lily pad, butterflies and frogs appear.

A procession of worshipers,
with a paladin of feast food, slide by,
a royal procession on horseback gallops over water,
bannered captains leading.

Suddenly
an explosion of Buddha babies splash
like synchronized swimmers
boats full of elegant passengers float in,
followed by dragons, who dance, battle, exit again
and the curtain rises.

Puppeteers, up to their waists in water,
garbed in rich silk trousers and tops,
come forward, clap and are clapped.

The music stops,
we wander out:
mystified.

Ho Chi Minh Mausoleum

Sunday packs it with the curious and the reverential:

Bureaucracy: the power of the whistle and he who holds it
shrilly greets my pause before the former Presidential Palace
thwarts my would be corner-cutting
parade ground seven blocks long.
"Forward," whistle and pointed finger scream.

Past long, shady embassy row,
Marxist friends close—
Poland, East Germany, Albania—
past yellow-gold three-storied Foreign Affairs
prescribed French-Indochinese era architecture
Chinese tile roof and garrotes
red iron balconies, green window shutters.

Around huffing buses unloading visitors
to the entrance
to a cascade of covered walkways and narrow pavilions
a white uniformed army staff every few feet,
the wide-screened TV projections:

silk-clad women, uniformed soldiers,
plump-checked children sing
paens to the Great Leader,
accompany each step.
Past security, once, twice, seven times,
into the labyrinth of courtyards
leading to the inner sanctum

Put in pairs,
we walk in total silence,
hands down, solemn,
then exit
at the stark stone mausoleum,
pass more guards
mount internal stairs

Pause,
take steps to circumambulate
the sunken, encased form,
Ho Chi Minh, his familiar narrow chin
covered by wispy white goatee,
surreally revitalized yearly
by those who do Lenin in Moscow.

Is there defiance in his afterlife,
this man who skirted the material,
lived simply, wanted to be cremated,
have his ashes scattered from the riversides
all over his land?

He asked for equity, stayed in a stilt house,
bamboo edging a simple lake
worked in a book-shelved office,
filled up a garage with used cars
on the edge of the palace
he never lived in.

Would he applaud the massive black museum
showing minutia of his life, writings and studies,
the French Communist Party
leading the revolution
against the cruel French-Indochinese War,
independence on this site in 1954?

Was it his words made flesh
in distaste for U.S. imperialism
modern capitalism, believing it would fall
at the hands of educated people—
as one sculpture shows
a Ford Edsel smashing through a wall
symbolizing how the U.S. system,
in industry and warfare, would fail?

Reality enshrined, the dislike,
in practices, the antithesis.

We dare not shuffle nor linger,
just view, honorific, silent,
then exit into sunshine,
retrieve possessions,
                and go on.

SAPA

Raw,
rolling from the night on the train out of Hanoi,
then lifted with dawn from the border town of Cao Bai
up mountains chiseled
with dissolving bands of green rice terraces
we climb to our hotel in Sapa,
build above the valley like a birdhouse.

Like a French Alps village in summer,
grand-old dame sandstone and brick mansions,
terraced and balconied, stand above
a central square, lake, and cathedral on the hill.
From our wraparound hotel bedroom
we look out at water buffalos, fat-bellied pigs,
terraces flowing down the valley and up hills
to forested peaks, Ho and Lien.

The ethnic women-Hmong, Zao, Dao,
Red Zao, Black Hmong—swarm, selling,
black-bloused, thick skeins of hair pinned up,
black leg bands tight,
their scarves and shawls broadcast
ancient geometric figures and stripes
like those carved by their millennium-aged ancestors
on these rocks themselves.

They sell or embroider in the sun in the square below.
I shake them off like fresh water
to walk up Dragon Jaw's hill,
broad stairs climbing past shops
selling herbs, mushrooms, funghi
dried and pickled fruits and vegetables.

In the Garden of the Clouds,
the Orchid and Western and Four Seasons gardens
fields of porous limestone wind-carved into otherworld shapes
abut pine trees and gravestones.
On a platform overlooking the valley
a young Black Dao women, baby strapped to her back,
startles me: What is this slight beauty.
doing up here alone on the high perch?

At dusk the mountains settle in thick clouds
mist and shadow tunnel our eyes,
through layers of light,
smoky illusions, only their outline,
ridges profound and solid
under Fanespan

The Hmong, Dao women
mount the hills
return to villages
where terraced fields
unroll great steps
carved out for centuries
by their walkings.

In our hotel room,
all night the pipes and strings vibrate
waft up from the winding street.
As the wind blows, shutters slap,
the whole room rolls,
visited by the walking dead, hungry ghosts
who rattle the panes,
roil the balcony and shriek,

only the ladies' thin wooden amulets,
and local poltergeists,
protect us from 10,000 years
of magic.

THE DZAO AND HMONG

❧ ❧

This is Ta Phin,
a Black Dzao and Hmong village:

creased like a shut fist among tiny gardens
it seems Potemkin:
empty shop fronts, open wooden shelters,
only a hand-packed path leading up to a cave
haunted by the guerrillas
who first tunneled through the mountains
back to Cai, to fight the French.

Bees in a swarm, the tiny ladies
cheer us when we step down,
tackle, attach, one per tourist.
Heavy carved silver necklaces,
bracelets and earrings jangling,
weighing them down, they follow
us close the hamlet's length, then back.

I warrant two escorts.
They take my name like secretaries,
smile toothlessly, then hold me back
over and over,
to offer for obligatory sale
their embroidered bags
shawls, belts, and baby hats.

I study the long hair tucked up
in large red turbans, like pillows
or gigantic headache balls
the hair above the forehead shaved,
emboldening their old eyes,
the indigo-dyed line clothing, shirts, aprons,
retro leggings, cylindrical hats, that mark their tribe.

I think of the Hmong resettled to
Minneapolis after Vietnam,
wonder if they still are animists,
use folk medicines, worship ancestors,
perform *ban ho*
with ritual pigs and chickens
in tall St. Paul public housing?

Way ahead, back in the van,
my fellow travels huddle,
smirking at me, the only American
among the practical Brits
and their Commonwealth:
I buy from all three ornate ladies,
then flee.

Thousands of miles away, in my own home,
I open the crafts and sound their artistry,
the intricate embroidered patterns and minute stitches,

know nothing wasted, none overpriced,
know a small justness in
my own purse being emptied
to fill the ladies'.

SAPA HIKE AND WATERFALLS

Around the edges of terraced rice fields
through villages of wooden houses
perched on rolling hills,
accompanied by a pied piper of vendors,
our local craftswomen, we hike.

On route to the waterfall
named by locals for the fish who leaped
out of the water in the old days,
brooks trickle down bamboo cylinders
channeled into paddies.

Along the Lavie Stream, in dry season
the boulders look like lions and dragons,
praying pigs, butterflies.
In rainy season, splashing water births
purple iris, pink and yellow lilies.

That night in Ta Van, a tiny hamlet,
we sleep and wake among the Dzao
in a large wood-frame lodge
with lofts head-to-toe with sleep gear,
dressed in mosquito nets.

Frances Garrett Connell

At dawn the roosters
prance and crow across the valley,
seeping water sounds like bells or subtle flute
among the wind's dawn breath
and distant traffic.

Stooping under backpacks
well-groomed schoolboys begin their trek:
in each house along the road,
fires are lit, children fed,
tasks unwound,

like long balls of yarn.

ILLUSION IN THE SAPA HILLS

Scarcely four feet tall,
these tiny girthed hill people

wind stirring the trees
delicate as a large hand, sudden,
fickle as a betraying lover

miniature limestone carvings
fanciful and intricate,
shadow animals and fortresses

mammoth homely water buffalo
stretched out before the day's work
in a raised mud corral

bananas hanging off the palmed tree
like suggestive fecund goddesses
behind thatched and stilted dwellings.

Solid Hmong scythe, chisel, wheat harvester
as each leers, tears into
the hard soil of a scrub garden

bare-bottomed wonders
toddlers, dusty and snotty nosed
frolicking along the pathways

mist shrouding distant peaks
like jagged teeth, etching themselves
across the sky seconds before sunset

sassy waves, carefully woven terraces,
stepping stones like the Great Wall
or the Pyramid of Gaza multiplied.

In reality
the best one can do with illusion
is toss it back to the clouds.

HALONG BAY

❧ ❧

As the jewel-lit junks around us
settle into darkness
our own boat, this floating hotel, ripples,
a long shadow in the limestone-grottoed bay
where 2,000 islands chiseled by sea,
wind, hidden springs and rain,
float indifferently.

As the vessel chugs across water,
we sip fruit nectar in champagne glasses,
eat potatoes sculpted to roses,
carrots shaved to orange petunias,
tomatoes flowing like red fountains,
cucumber and carrot slivers
pasted to china plates
like painted artwork,
cornucopias of beef and vegetables,

calamari, breaded sea perch
pork in saffron sauce,
prawns hung from a wire cup
like petals of a flower,
fried spring rolls
stuffed with delicate morsels,
tofu in a rice and soy broth,
watermelon, dragonfruit,
pineapple, oranges, pears.

We've come here,
shuttled by dory from Hai Long City:
cacophonous boats and tiny dinghies
merchants with mini-grocery shops
squeeze between barges,
carry wood, coal, building equipment,
cut across to other bay towns
that lap beside fishing huts as tiny as bird cages
on stilts edging the water
where fishermen farm their edible delights.

In floating villages
fishing corrals form labyrinths
within the wharfs.
Standing in their boats, locals dip,
one after the other,
their rhythmic long oars,
plying the bay and its caves.

Tourists in kayaks, we push off to emerald lagoons,
staccato coast, steep rising stone islands
dressed in fir trees.
Beyond an overhanging cave,
we circle silently, pairs of oars
slipping in and out of velvet water
like stiff wings rising and falling in tandem
for downed birds.

At dawn the sun stares boldly
between lagoons and snake-skin rocking islands
evoking the myth of this "Bay of the Descending Dragons:"
Assisting earthlings against an invader
Mother Dragon scooped out the bay,
each child left behind
became one of the islands.

The wooden boats scatter across water
in two-tiered splendor:
like the ethereal fallen creatures
they were supposed to be,
these hoary cliffs and caves,
grotto-scoured mountain islands,
circle us.

In ancient vigil,
like bowed dragon wings,
the world digs deep, unknowable,
beneath cool and supportive waves.

HOI AN EXPLORED

Locals believed a monster ruled the earth—
head in Japan, stomach in Vietnam,
tail in India—
sent storms to plague the ports,
spun tsumanis, floods, earthquakes or fire.
So the people prayed, built pagodas on
the ancient Covered Bridge
two guardian dogs watch over:

blue and yellow-tiled roof
on the east a dog, monkeys on the west
honoring the Japanese and Chinese Emperors
born in these animals' years.

But catastrophes still came.

Before the Thu Ban River (Cai)
silted, too shallow for ships
Hoi An's warehouses spilled over
spices. silk, fabrics, paper,
porcelain, tea, sugar, and molasses.
Traders exchanged elephant tusks, beeswax,
mother of pearl, lacquer, sulfur and lead.
They rankled, fought over, sold, and transported

in ships bound for China, Japan, the Netherlands
Portugal, Spain, India, the Philippines,
Indonesia, Thailand, France, England,
the United States.

The riverside's abuzz with vendors,
colors slipping into eighty tiny stores
making jewelery and cloth
in old wooden merchant houses and shops.
Museums highlight shipping routes,
15th century ceramic masterpieces, medicinists
beside ornate community halls, pagodas, family chapels,
assembly places for the maritime trade,
mansions once housing 18 generations,
always keeping a room above the rafters
to protect reliquaries,
when the river rose.

A walking museum for antique collectors,
water-brewed wooden houses
line narrow streets
where tailors, jewelers. lantern makers,
shoemakers and carvers,
recreate anything from a picture,
quickly, on the spot:
suits, rings, dresses, sandals, purses,

racing against time
machines, hands, catalogs whirring
they replicate any period, any item,
satisfy any request with artisan standards.

School children pedal home,
boys in blue caps, white scarves and shorts
older girls luminous as white candles
in *ao dai,* elegant white tunics.
Old men with faces like shattered clay masks
minute women in black pajamas, cone hats, bunned hair,
carry yokes full of everything:
rice, scrap metal, clay figurine whistles.

In architecture tradition and protocol prevail:
shopkeepers insert horizontal planks into grooves
that cut into the columns that support the roof,
to shutter shop fronts at night

A thousand brick-colored *an* and *duong*
(yin and yang) roof tiles alternate rows,
concave and convex tiles
securely fitted together,
they grow green in the monsoon season
when lichen and moss between tiles
burst into full life

To protect the residents from harm,
over each doorway round pieces of wood
surrounded by a spiral form an *om-duong*
the "door eyes," called *mat cua.*

On the waterside promenade,
colonnaded houses painted French colonial's
de *rigeur* mustard yellow, still prance,
lead to the alley where water flows,
for making *cao lau,*
doughy flat noodle with croûtons, bean spouts, greens,
topped with pork slices,
caught in crispy rice paper.

Then, inside a narrow wooden house,
under the gray-burnished planks,
resides to this day
the Department of Managing
and Gathering Swallow Nests:
twice a year, its officers grade and sell
nests collected off the coast
in the Cham Island archipelago

These strands of gummy saliva,
air-hardened,
make delicate soup:

and stimulate love.

SOLITUDE IN A LAST DAY,
HO CHI MINH CITY

Just blocks away from the Opera,
the Rex Hotel war-correspondent's haunted,
by shops selling model sailing ships

I sip Lipton tea atop a corner restaurant
near the Post Office:
the sprinkler hose sprays from balcony's edge,
attendants worry over rich pho dishes
as fried rice and ginger,
fish broth and cellulite noodles,
waft upward.

Against torpor, heat, a sleepless night
I give in to a tuna sandwich and iced chocolate milk
at the Perfect Cup, where young and coupled
Vietnamese nibble on their fortunes,
share laptops, sit heads close in
chatting, processing.

Later, showered, in thinner clothes,
I hike to the filthy Saigon River,
duck away from a rickshaw tracking my steps,
enter the Ton Duc Thong Museum
honoring Uncle Ton, colleague of Ho
co-founder of the worker's movement for Vietnam
Vice President of the reunited country
after liberation and the failed American War.

The massive villa in stages of repair
features scenes from French prisons
torture chambers, maps of centers of resistance,
photos, biography, clothes, letters,
household articles,
Uncle Ton's leather suitcase for missions.

Upstairs, I am the sole visitor:
a thin, huge brown-eyed girl
on her third day at work,
turns on the lights in three exhibit rooms,
coyly trails me as I feign interest
in the Lenin Prize given to this leader,
writings to an adopted daughter and son.

I bow, walk downstairs,
out past two docents
into a landscaped driveway
lined by guardhouses and motorbikes,
emerge on the boulevard
to find the rickshaw driver waiting.

At the Cathedral
I walk past three beggars on the steps,
limbs askew, settled like broken blocks.
Inside an elderly man
opens the grilled gate to the main section
marked "for prayers only."
I follow him to a pew beside
the chapel alcoves for different saints,
each wall naming the deceased,
admonishing Christ's mercy, God's grace
in Vietnamese and French.

TOURIST CIRCUIT ON THE MEKONG

Tin-roofed, porch-like shops
emerald paddies and cone-hatted farmers
weave between six-lane highways,
narrow control gate portals,
bamboo, banana and palm trees,
lead to a port, a tiny boat
to carry us across the Mekong.

Sipping on half-shells of coconut milk
we dock and thread over wooden planks
past water hyacinth trees
marked for German furniture,
to the coconut candy factory.

Production moves in single table stages:
groups cluster to hack off the exterior
reveal hairy next layer, juice and the fruit,
feed the machine that shreds the core
blend the pulp with caramel
spread the candy like fudge on huge sheets
cut it into pieces, nimbly wrapped,
so we can chew and purchase samples.

In dusty corners,
behemoths coil inside
rows of snake wine
adding fermentation,
to ripening rose, apple, banana,
guava, peanut brews.

Out on a shaded porch
a woman makes rice paper
over a raging fire,
the delicate round wafers dry on racks
strung up on lines
like albino leaves

At the end of a donkey-driven cart ride
to the other end of the delta village,
as school boys pedal home for lunch
under more palm and banana trees,

the master offers pots of tea and honey
from his hives, gives pats of royal gel
(for face and stomach)
offers platters of cut pomelo, pineapple
dragonfruit, and lychee nut,

then brings a python to pose beside us
its six feet looped around our necks
safe in the hands of one
born in the Year of the Snake.

Short trekked to the canoes
(this circuit imitating Disneyland's
"Pirates of the Caribbean"),
we are knighted with conical hats,
then punted along a lagoon
to our original small boat.

Frances Garrett Connell

At another wharf, a private restaurant
we share elephant ear fish
deep-fried and presented intact
on a stand-up rack.

The hostess shows the protocol:
dip rice paper in water
add squiggly white noodles,
Vietnamese morning glory lettuce,
parts of thyme,

then remove the tip spine, spear the fish
fold the moist white flesh inside

roll it all up and dip
in peanut mango coconut sauce.

Consume.

MEKONG DELTA

Beyond the swath of delta jungle,
huge billboards advertise
An Dean Kin's Coconut Candy
before the new river bridge
over the Mekong River.

I wake under mosquito-netted cot
on the edge of the canals riddling
the small farmyard and orchards
of this tiny village.

Geekos puff and squeak
in the banana and coconut trees
the omnipresent rooster crows and stalks

as tiny net hammocks sway—
hugging coconut-leaf palms
under the thatched roof pavilions
of our homestay host, lively Mrs Tan.

Last night's rats
who'd raced the rafter
over our feast table,
are silent,
as the fan circulates overhead
imperceptibly
with a cooling dawn breeze.

Frances Garrett Connell

We'd come from My Tho
via the chocolate rippling water,
the churning river as wide as a city
to the hamlet pathed and canal-threaded,
canopied with fruit trees

pungent, dangling jackfruit,
coconut, mangoes,
coca beans,
plums, small pineapple plants,
dragonfruit,
a paradise:

Fishermen make hoop-studded nets
to haul in the bounty
as sawmills buzz, gnawing through jungle.
Inside each house a TV runs,
a scooter stands taut.

Beside well-watered vegetable plots
the commune children
play with strings and balls.

WALKING HO CHI MINH CITY AND
THE WAR REMNANTS MUSEUM

Shedding the dark veranda's cool,
I step out into searing sun
like the gauze masks some motorbikers don,
imagine French vowels soaring, lisping intrigue
when the teak-wooded floors
housed coffee and hostelry,
hosted an Indochinese empire.

In Saigon, ruthless to walkers,
honking, polluting scooters, cabs
race in unbreaking streams
down every lane, boulevard or rue
as commerce spills onto curbs
over narrow sidewalks.

At shoulder-to-shoulder shops
as random as a twister's debris,
families, neighbors nibble, serve breakfast,
on miniature plastic chairs and tables,
wield water buckets to lay down the dust,
wet towels to throw over heads
or sooth burning eyes.

Scooter rental shops, parking spots, sprawl,
closet-size stands spill out rowed books,
cards, boxed merchandise,
hawkers scream under sandwich boards
or clutch in hand or under shirt,
billfolds, books, sunglasses,
stamps, postcards equal to a day's wages.

To walk to any place,
is to give your life to their hands.
Weaving, you progress,
each time you cross
your body a trajectory
against chaos and speed.

Initially unticketed,
then chitted,
at the fenced museum
I enter first a dirt yard
its hard baked surfaces
like clotted milk
littered with downed weaponry:

U.S. Army and Air Force helicopters
fighter planes, tanks rotund with history,
dusty, rusted like artifacts of a dead empire,
a litany of death:
UH-1 "Huey" helicopter,
F-5A fighter BLU-82 "Daisy Cutter" bomb,
M48 Patton tank, A-1 attack bomber.

Inside, the children's art display
vibrates hearts, birds, and rainbows,
school kids holding hands
themed "peace with all nations."

Another wall punctures my eyes,
a mournful sculpture of a shattered mother
bends beside the photographs of atrocities:

charred remnants, taut bagged bones
like a disemboweled jackrabbit,
a Viet Cong soldier hangs from "the grunt's" arm;
three GIs hover with water torture hose
over a stretched out captive,
in another, Marines drag a Vietcong
chained from behind a military wagon
as his skin tears off.
Beside, horror, harrowing, Bob King,
Lt. Calley's massacres,
photographs of mutilated children
burned bodies, napalmed limbs
persecution camps,
stacked body bags.

Agent Orange thick clouds like jet streams,
pulse from a U.S. Air Force plane
skimming rice fields and jungle, defoliating.
Melded and misshaped flesh and bone—
victims of dioxin, agent orange—stare back.

Ten years "Operation Ranch Hand,"
sprayed 20 million gallons of the poison
in Vietnam, Laos and Cambodia
inducing famine, killing, maiming 400,000,
generating 500,000 children with birth defects—
cleft palates, mental retardation, hernias,
swollen heads, extra fingers and toes—
affecting three million.
Dioxin lasts centuries:
(39,000 U.S. Vets made claims,
486 were compensated.)

Upstairs display cases flash with familiar faces:
Lodge, McNamara, Westmoreland,
Nixon, Johnson mouthing lies, strategies,
protesters marching crowded streets
worldwide against the war,
international war-correspondents
recording truth, or martyred.

Maps chart the battles:
percentage of mined lands,
places defoliated,
pounds of armaments, bombs, artillery dropped,
numbers of French, then U.S. and allied troops,
interspersed with lines from
the Geneva Conference
international treaties,
Ho Chi Minh's objectives.

Three million Vietnamese dead,
two million injured, half a million lost,

other numbers never posted on these walls:
58,000 American, thousands of allies' deaths,
millions made refugees,
killed in reeducation campaigns,
Laotian Royals and civilians
under the Pathet Lao,
Cambodians in Civil War,
two million from Khmer genocide

Seven million lives
taken by human hands
in sun

in shadow.

For what.

TOURISTS IN THE IMPERIAL CAPITAL

ಅಲ್ ೕಲ

At Hue, on the Perfume River,
we mount a double dragon-headed platoon.

Each leaps aboard:
the svelte, soon-to-be-wedded English MD,
a pudgy boyish Irish geologist,
his tall carriage horse racer friend,
the pair of graying Vancouver hippies,
enthusiastic children in a toy store
at every venture,

our witty English actuary,
his stoic child-psychologist wife,
then the female Albertians—solid counselor,
ethno-musicologist, research physician,
petite, sullen French teacher—
followed by the six foot four Dutch child,
at 22 the youngest and most traveled.

Our guide, Ha, jumps over,
the owner poles us out,
a Vietcong veteran's son,
his laxness in sharing itinerary details
earned this trip the title
"Magical Mystery Tour."
Slowly the vessel moves up river, south
to realms of old Emperors' graves.

We follow narrow planks to the bank,
path through hillsides clutching vegetable gardens,
a street exploding colors from local painters,
incense, fans, libation stands,
to the Tomb of Tu Duc
high-walled, pine-wooded sanctuary,
with lake-side pavilion where he wrote poetry,
watched his concubines dance.

Husband to 148 wives, he was sterile,
adopted an heir, who committed suicide,
boasted a theater, residences,
honorary temples for mother and favorite wives,
built a classical Chinese tomb
whose rows of animals and warriors line a plaza
where his actual body was never interred.

The puffing dragon splashes on
to the 400 year-old Thien Mu Pagoda:
yellow-robed boy monks in training
sound the drums, ting bells and chant,
the bonsai garden expectant with
frangipani trees, gigantic magnolia-rich blossoms
already in the puffy clouds overhead.

From here, in June 1963, the monk Thich Quang Duc
drove to Saigon, and self-immolated
protesting the wicked Diem government's
persecution of Buddhists,
the flaming man pictured around the world
as good Catholic Madame Diem
shrugged off "Buddhist barbecues."

Back on the river,
the boat putters upstream
past quiet fishermen, other families
running dragon-headed tourist boats.
Men mine for sand mid-river,
school boys dare each other
to swim across shallow shoals.

Ha tells me of the weeping veterans,
sons of the Midwest, he led once.
They only knew their combat zones
by numbered places on tattered
military maps they clutched:
all ears, eyes and memories.

Beside Hue's purple ruins
I am not colored by bruises,
but history:
the only American along.

VIII

FOR WHAT IS REAL

For What is Real

၆၃ ၈၃

"The selfsame word can at one time be the cornerstone of peace, while at another machine-gun fire resounds in every syllable."
    Vaclav Havel

Fathomless, huge eyes dart,
dark as sweet, crushed blackberries.
She prattles about an imaginary Indian sister's braided hair,
schools for "grouchy Daddy" to learn gentleness,
pink-clad princesses disappearing with a silver slipper's click,
her real brother, just beyond his first steps,
who grins and pulls down the curtains again and again.
All the while she spins on ballerina toes
snipping to tiny scraps
old wrapping paper and magazine pictures I give her:

What her mother labels junk, I call her treasures.

At thee-and-a-half, already an irreplaceable, irrepressible person,
she cruises a white flying horse through phantom clouds,
tugs a slip of kite into the Hudson breeze,
flings thick black ringlets above narrow shoulders,
then dashes off to drench herself in the park's water spray,
to race in perfect balance up Manhattan schist mountains,
feral and boundless.

One grandparent an illiterate Tibetan healer,
another a long-dead village monk,
the third and fourth a German-Czech farmer's daughter,
and an iconoclastic pacifist born at the start of the last century:
passions and spirits cavort deep in the electric bones
of this tiny tense receptacle of continents and centuries.

What one man calls trash and superstition,
another calls miracles and God.

In Waziristan, drones lacerate mountain compounds,
slicing a mother and her sleeping child,
as a despot gases his rebellious citizens,
1300 frothing, dying outside Damascus.
Thinking to avoid HIV, or just subhuman,
men rape toddler girls in Uganda, India, the Congo,
while Wall Street ventures compound rich men's empires
gambling away a generation's livelihood with shoddy gold.
In China's Shanxi province, coal spews, blackening the sky,
children pick through toxic computer parts in Guiyu,
in Kambata, Ethiopia climate refugees starve.
High in sky-arched Himalayan valleys,
millennium-patient glaciers melt.

The all-consuming locusts of humanity ignore what is real.
What greedy leaders, soporific citizens manifest,
nature suffers us to take away, to end a fragile spaceship's glide
in galaxies of lifeless ice and fire and unbirthed words.

Climb, climb, little Angelika.
Dance away doom.

ACKNOWLEDGMENTS

Thanks to my family for giving me the space to finish these projects, for the gracious apartment in 790 Riverside which lent me stability and distance, to the libraries and Alumnae associations of Barnard College and Columbia University which provided resources.

The following poems in this collection have been published elsewhere:

"Dark Soul I" (*Rockhurst Review* Spring 2012)
"Prose Poem after the Greeks, Draft One"(Saranac Review, Issue 8, 2012)
"Excerpts from "Le Gare St-Lazare:" After the Painting by Manet (*The Grey Sparrow,* Summer 2013)
"Amber" (*The Grey Sparrow,* Summer 2013)
"Drinking Fountain"(*The Grey Sparrow,* Summer 2013)
"'Among the Quadi, on the River Oien'" (*Picayune,* Spring 2012)
"Drunken Squirrels" (*Pinyon,* Spring 2012)

ABOUT THE AUTHOR

A graduate of Barnard College, with a masters from University of Virginia and a doctorate from Columbia, mother of three amazingly diverse and well-traveled and well-read sons, Frances Connell has been published in more than two dozen literary magazines and anthologies, including *Pig Anthology, Baltimore Review, Potomac Review, Negative Capability, Monocacy Valley Review,* and *Excursis,* and in the *Washington Post,* and *The Christian Science Monitor.* In addition to previously teaching writing, oral history and international development at the University of Pennsylvania, Kabul University, St. Mary's Seminary and University (Baltimore), George Mason University, and Montgomery College, and running refugee resettlement programs in the Maryland and D.C. area, she currently teaches for the University of Maryland University College. During graduate and undergraduate studies, she worked with Elizabeth Hardwick, Peter Taylor, Joy Chute, Alan Williamson, and more recently participated in small poetry workshops with Sarah Cotterill and Marvin Gavin. She has three books currently available at http://www2.xlibris.com/bookstore/author.aspx?authorid=9207: *The Rest is Silence: Poems; Down Rivers of Windfall Night* (novel), and *Children Kept from the Sun.* She is completing another novel, a collection of travel poems, and a nonfiction book on Afghanistan in the late 1970's, and currently lives in New York City.

The End

The End